FOREVER YOUNG

A MOTHER'S STORY OF L

CW00797021

By Sharon Truesdale

With Sue Leonard

The Authors

Sharon Truesdale studied law before becoming a qualified youth worker, currently working in the area of special education. She is the mother of Matthew, who died by suicide aged 17, and of Natasha, Annie-Jean and Daniel. She lives in County Antrim, Northern Ireland.

A journalist and ghost writer, **Sue Leonard** is the co-author of two recent number one bestsellers: ***Whispering Hope***: The True Story of the Magdalene Women (Orion 2015) and ***An Act of Love*** with Marie Fleming, recounting Marie's extraordinary life and fight for the right to die with dignity. (Hachette Ireland, 2014). She has worked on five other books as a ghost writer, two, for Penguin Ireland were best sellers. Sue is the author of ***Keys to the Cage*** (New Island, 2010)

Remembering Matthew James Truesdale

3rd April 1995 – 11 October 2012

'Loved and Remembered Everyday'

Preface

On October 11th, 2012, my son, Matthew, hung himself in his bedroom. In that moment, everything changed. The old Sharon Truesdale died along with seventeen-year-old Matthew, and the new one struggled to find a way to live. Dragging myself through the first difficult hours, days, weeks and months, I learned that grief was a roller-coaster ride. Opening my eyes each day, I never knew what to expect. This book is for anyone who, like me, thinks that through their grief, they are going mad.

Suicide, in Northern Ireland, is all too common. In 2012, when Matthew died, there were 318 registered deaths by suicide in Northern Ireland, (though some of these died earlier.) And in the 10 years before that, deaths by suicide averaged 274, so there are many other grieving relatives.

I've written this book to help others who, like me, had never experienced a loss, or understood what grief actually was. The existing books I read which highlighted the stages of grief made some sense, yet my feelings, actions and behaviours seemed extreme. Was that because losing a child to suicide made my experience more traumatic? I don't know.

Every day I wondered how I was going to survive until nightfall living with the immense pain I carried, thinking, always, of the moment that I found my son. Would the pain ever lessen? What did it all mean?

The book is also a celebration of Matthew's short life – and explores the elements that led him to take this drastic step. And I look at the services available to him, and how they fell short. Had different measures been taken, could my son have been saved?

Prologue.

I awoke, as usual, to the beep of my alarm clock. It was six-thirty on Thursday 11th October, and it was time to get up for work, but, zapping the alarm, I didn't move. I'm a disciplined person, and my routine, every day, is to leap out of bed – cross the corridor and wake my younger daughter, Annie Jean, then my elder one, Natasha, so that they'll be ready for school. But that morning I could not move. Something wasn't right.

The alarm was set to snooze, and every seven minutes it beeped its impatience. Each time, muffling it, I continued to lie there, staring at the ceiling, noticing, with irritation, a cobweb in the corner. It wasn't until the clock said seven twenty-one that I realised I simply *must* get up. I thought, if I don't, I'll be late for work.

I didn't go and wake the girls. I've no idea why. Instead, breaking my routine, I made for the stairs. Normally, the first thing I do when I get downstairs is switch on the kettle. But not that day. Instead, bypassing it, I opened the door and let out Buster, our new puppy. Then I made my way towards Matthew's room, a specially converted garage. I've no idea why. At 17, Matthew had left school. He had a job, but as he started at nine, was able to sleep until 8.0'clock. All I know is that when I opened the door, everything changed. And changed forever.

I could see straight into Matthew's room; and I saw him, my firstborn son, sitting at the foot of his four-poster bed. He was staring straight at me, his dark brown eyes fixed, his head at an unnatural angle. And I knew, instinctively, that he was dead. Fearful, I stood as still as a sculpture. Frozen; my eyes fixed on him.

'What have you done Matthew,' I whispered. 'I'm trained in first aid, but I can't help you. I can't help you if you're not breathing.' It was obvious that he had strangled or hung himself, and though I was horrified, I didn't scream. I couldn't.

Had I suspected something was wrong? Was that why I had stayed lying in bed – to put off the moment when my life would change? I don't know the answer to that.

I went calmly up the stairs, collected Annie-Jean, and brought her into my bedroom. Then I collected Natasha. 'Don't go downstairs,' I said. 'Just stay here.' Did they ask me why? Did they wonder why I wasn't shouting at them to get ready for school? I can't remember, but I didn't tell them about Matthew. And I didn't cry. How could I, when I was frozen in time?

Downstairs again, I rang 999. 'My son is dead,' I said, when a woman's voice answered. 'He killed himself.' My words sounded flat and remote – it was as if my voice had detached itself from my emotions.

'Do you want an ambulance?'

I thought, what a stupid question. Hadn't she heard what I said? 'I don't think an ambulance will help.'

'Would you like the police to come?'

I sighed. I could no more make decisions at that moment than dance a gig. 'Just send who you want,' I said. 'Nothing can help him now.'

PART ONE: BEFORE

1

How it Started

From the first time I saw Matthew – from the time I first held him in my arms, it's always been him and me. It was brilliant having a baby boy, the first grandchild. He was just my boy. The baby I had hoped and planned for.

Whatever happened afterwards; whatever we both went through; it was us against the world. I never doubted that. A few months before he died, when his girlfriend asked him who he loved most in the whole world, she expected him to say it was her; but he said he loved me best; his mum.

I was equally smitten with Matthew's dad James when I first caught sight of him. I was nineteen years old with my whole life ahead of me, and everything seemed possible. I was in Sleepers Nightclub in Antrim with Julie, a friend since primary school, and it was *the* place to be on a Saturday night. Julie saw him first. 'Don't look now,' she said, 'but there's a guy over there who can't take his eyes off you.'

Of course, I looked over straight away, and she was right. This handsome, dark haired guy was staring at me, and when he noticed me looking at him, his face relaxed into a huge grin. He sauntered over with a swagger and told me his name was James. He was lovely! Easy to talk to, and charming. I noticed other – prettier – girls giving him the eye, and I couldn't believe he had chosen me.

We arranged to spend the next evening together, and from then on, we were inseparable. James was working for the Antrim Council at the time, doing garden maintenance. We'd meet in his lunchbreak, and would wander around, holding hands.

We spent the whole summer together. I had been in Middlesbrough, in the North of England for the past year. I was studying law at Teesside University, but was considering chucking it in, a decision that seemed inevitable after I'd met James. I was enjoying the course but had found it hard to make friends. I'm half Chinese – and there, away from my family, I felt that nobody accepted me. As I wasn't white, I wasn't accepted into the white community – but I wasn't accepted into the Chinese community either. And at the end of the summer, I couldn't bear the thought of leaving James and going back to that loneliness. It would be so much harder now that I had someone to miss. I thought James was my saviour.

I expected James to be happy for me to stay, but he surprised me.

'Don't rush into a decision,' he said. 'You worked so hard to get on that course; it would be a shame to chuck it all now.'

I think he was proud of me, and felt it reflected well on him to have a university going girlfriend.

'What would you do instead?' he asked me.

I laughed. 'I haven't a clue,' I said, and that's when he had his bright idea.

'Go back,' he said. 'Finish your course, but I'll come too.'

I laughed. 'But you've got your job here.'

'Yeah, but that's not for long,' he said. 'My contract runs out at the end of the month. I might as well look for a job in England as back here.'

It was decided. We travelled together and found some accommodation. And if my heart sank when I saw the tiny bedsit, which had a sink and cooker, but only just enough room for a sofa-bed, I didn't care. Even the thought of sharing a toilet and shower didn't daunt me. I had James, and that was all that mattered.

Another couple lived upstairs, and I'd thought, maybe, they'd become friends, but that wasn't to be. They had a volatile relationship to say the least – and it was clear that he was an abuser. Our lives were punctuated by the sound of him beating her, and of her screaming. One night, after they'd had a particularly noisy fight, a police car drew up. Watching the flashing lights through the thin curtains, I wondered, aloud, who has reported the domestic, and waited to hear the police stomp up the stairs. But the footsteps stopped on our floor and went along the corridor.

'We've a search warrant,' they said, and it turned out that this quiet guy who kept himself to himself, had got himself into a spot of bother. The police were checking for stolen items, and after that, they became frequent callers to the building. None of this mattered to me. I felt safe with James.

I settled down better at college, too. Nothing seemed so bad now that James was with me. He was happy too. He found work in an elderly care home, and it suited him. He's such a charmer, and that smile would light anyone's day. He loved the old people, and they, in return, seemed to love him. When he talked of them, and told me of their past lives, his face would soften. He wasn't earning much – there was enough for us to live on, but I was paying college fees, so I got a part-time job with the Royal Mail, and that helped to see us through.

At Christmas, when James asked me to marry him, I jumped at the chance and said, 'yes.' It was everything I wanted. Every time I looked at the beautiful emerald and diamond engagement ring, he'd bought me, I felt like the luckiest girl in the world.

'Let's just go away and do it!' he said. 'Let's go to Cyprus. Then we just do it quietly.'

Kissing him, I agreed. It seemed like the most romantic thing in the world! So, we booked the tickets.

James's sister Eleanor, and my elder sister Kathy were my bridesmaids, and Gary, Eleanor's boyfriend, acted as best man. A friend of Kathy's came, but there were no other guests – we didn't need anyone else - but I wanted tradition.

'I have to have a white dress,' I said. I'd been dreaming of a white wedding since I was small. I bought a beautiful white wedding dress, and felt I was floating on air! I'd chosen purple striped dresses for the bridesmaids. The colour complemented them all.

Making my vows, looking into James's eyes, I felt an overwhelming sense of happiness. I hadn't the slightest doubt that I was doing the right thing. The *only* thing. Nothing else made sense. I was 20. I loved James, and believed he was the only man for me. I wanted to be married to him, and I longed for a family.

I passed my exams in the summer and James was still happy in his job, so instead of returning home, we decided to stay put. My brother came over to join us. We had a wonderful time. But at the end of the summer holidays, when my brother had returned home, and I was due back at university, something had changed. I was homesick and decided not to stay. This time James didn't try to dissuade me. We were now married!

That was all very well, but where were we to live? We'd decided to stay in Northern Ireland, but we hadn't thought beyond the wedding and had no concrete plans. When we started looking for somewhere to live, we became disheartened.

'We can't afford it, James,' I said. 'What are we going to do?'

'We could live with my mother,' he said, and reluctantly, I agreed. And that's when the honeymoon ended.

We both found jobs – mine with the Royal Mail sorting office in Belfast – and James worked as a welder in Fruehauf, Newtownabbey. James's mother, Joyce, spoilt us. I'd come home and find dinner on the table, and our bed made.

The trouble was, that, being under his childhood roof, James's behaviour changed. Bad memories surfaced for him. He'd never got on with his dad. He craved his father's attention but ended up getting regularly beaten; it was his sister, Ann-Marie who his dad loved. Sensing this, trying to make things better, his mum spoiled James. It was a toxic combination. There were stories; stories that made my hair stand on end.

I came to realise that Joyce hadn't had an easy time of it either. She eventually left Jim, James's dad, but he had always treated her badly, and she had accepted this as normal because she truly loved him. I suppose it was a sign of the times, but it came as a terrible shock to me.

One day, when I got home from work, Joyce poured me a cup of tea, and sat down with me at the kitchen table. Something in her expression made me realise there was something important she wanted to say to me.

'Sharon,' she said. 'A wife has certain duties. And one of them is to agree to have sex whenever her husband wants it. If she doesn't, she has no one to blame if he looks for it elsewhere.'

I looked at her, open mouthed. It so happened that the night before James wanted sex and I didn't, but how did she know I'd turned him down? Had he told her? Surely not! Blushing with mortification, I said, 'Last night we had an argument. We weren't talking.' Under my breath, I added, 'not that it's any of your business.'

'It doesn't matter,' she said. 'Argument or not, a wife should give her husband sex. A man has certain needs.'

Astonished, I simply walked away. Or tried to. But she followed me out of the kitchen and told me that she never turned Jim down. 'You think you have it tough, but I'm telling you. My Jim slept with other women, and even so, I never turned him down. And one day he picked up an infection.'

'What? You mean an STI?' I shuddered.

'Indeed. And do you think I turned him away?'

'You didn't?' I widened my eyes. Was she for real?

I found James lying in front of the TV. Assuming he'd overheard the end of Joyce's advice, I muttered, 'What was *that* about? Did you tell her about last night?'

Flicking channels, he didn't answer, but he coloured.

Another night, I came home, and couldn't find my hairbrush. It wasn't on the dressing-table as normal. Looking for it, I noticed that everything had been moved – and some ornaments were missing. I couldn't understand it. 'Oh yes,' said Joyce when I brought it up. 'I had a little tidy-up. You don't mind?'

I stared at her. 'I left the room tidy this morning. It's just that everything has moved.'

She didn't say anything, but I saw her glance over at James.

'What?'

James picked up his jacket, and walked out of the house, slamming the door behind him.

I turned to Joyce. 'What happened?' I wasn't going to let this go. And, finally, she told me. 'Poor James,' she said. 'He had a bad day at work.'

'And?'

'He's frustrated,' she said. 'He deserves something better.'

'He wrecked the room, didn't he?'

'That's men for you,' she said, nodding, and I felt a knot of dread in my stomach.

The more I learned of Joyce's old-fashioned views, the more astonished I became. She believed, sincerely, that a woman's place was in the home, at the kitchen sink. Sometime later, she let slip her view that married women should not work. She virulently disapproved of those in a male role – like a woman ambulance driver.

Over the years, however, I began to appreciate that Joyce was a dedicated mother who was simply a woman of her time. And she did change, when her daughters entered the workplace. I was astonished the day she entered it herself! She worked in Muckamore Pre-School Nursery, the one Matthew would attend, and helped distract him, when he tried to follow his other nana – my mum, out of the school.

Whenever James brought up the subject of his father, and of the many rows and beatings, I expressed shock. But James would just shrug as if this was normal. Then he'd point out that I hadn't much experience of fathers. And that was true. Mine had left my mother when I was just ten years old.

He had an affair and simply abandoned us. One day he was there; the next he had gone. We'd recently moved from Chester to Northern Ireland; my dad was in the army, so we were always being uprooted. Mum was bitter. Having been offered security by the army for so many years, it felt especially tough being abandoned by them too, with no help or support.

He left us on the Springfarm Estate – which, whilst originally used to house army families, was now also taking in civilians. Being Chinese, we didn't fit in. It's not just that there were no Chinese families around then – I never met any mixed-race children either. She never forgave my father. She sank into a torpor, and then into deep depression. At 10, I didn't understand what had been going on, but I remember the whispers before we'd moved.

I also remember arriving at St Patrick's Barracks in Ballymena; I remember all our boxes stacked around the rooms. Mum was happy at this fresh start; she'd known that Dad had had an affair, but he'd assured her that it was now over. But one day, emptying his jacket pockets before she sent it to the cleaners, she came across a letter.

Mum could speak some English – but she could neither read nor write, so she took the letter to a neighbour. Imagine her horror when the neighbour read it, and she realised she'd been deceived once again. The affair was still going on. Horrified, she went to the officer in charge to tell him the marriage was over. I imagine she'd expected a sympathetic ear, along with some support but she got neither. She was made an outcast.

I missed my dad. I missed him terribly. I blamed him for leaving and I hated him for that. How could he abandon us – and it was an abandonment in every sense. The army life is simple. You move from house to house, but the basics for living were provided. You'd have furniture, pots and pans and bedclothes. And if the blankets were itchy, at least they kept you warm.

There's a lot to be said for living within a closed camp. It gave us security, friends, and things to do; there were youth clubs, and activities, and all away from the civilian world outside the barriers, which was deemed unsafe.

When Dad left, we were provided with a house from the Northern Ireland Housing Executive, but it came unfurnished. All we had at the start were two wooden chairs that the painters had left behind.

It was a bleak time. Mum didn't believe in loans, so we had no sofa until she could afford to pay for it. She didn't realise, at first, that she was entitled to anything, because in Singapore, where she came from, there was no benefit system. If your family didn't help you, you had to work. And when work was scarce, the family shared. When my uncle, who was a welder, got a contract on the ships for a year, he saved and supported the extended family. As jobs were shared his contract would be given to someone else. Then it was somebody else's turn. That was the accepted way of things.

Life improved, a little, when Mum's solicitor's secretary, Betty, helped her to claim benefits. Throughout all this time, Mum looked amazing. She wore tight jeans with high heel shoes, and her red lipstick and sunglasses gave her an air of glamour and confidence. When we walked through the town, people turned their heads to watch her. I remember, one day, sitting on a bench with her, and this fellow came up and started chatting to her. She lit up at the attention, but it was years before she trusted a man again.

Nobody seeing her strutting around town would guess that she had any problems to contend with. But the truth was we had lost our mother to depression. She was in a very bad way. Returning from school one day, there was a strange woman in the house. 'I'm from social services,' she said.

'Does you mum have any tablets' She asked, and I said that yes, she had.

'Can you show me where she keeps them?'

I did so, and now, wonder if they thought she was suicidal. And I wonder, was she? Had she been considering taking her life? I don't know the answer to that. What I do know, is that her depression made her angry, and that I was the one to get the brunt of her anger. Whilst my sister and brother got away scot free, I was blamed for everything. One day I asked her why. 'You're your dad's favourite,' she said. That made me wonder if I reminded her of him.

I was eleven before I realised that I was 'different.' I'd started Antrim High School. It was a shock. The girls would shout, 'chinky.' It could have been a lonely time, but I had a friend!

On my first day, I walked into the classroom and noticed a beautiful girl with long blonde hair. There was a spare seat beside her. I sat there, and my friendship with Jacqueline began. We hadn't any other friends, not really. At first, we played with Julie, who'd also moved here from Springfarm Primary school, but as time went on, she started smoking, and moving with a new crowd. We didn't care. We didn't need anyone else. We'd play chase in the playground, taking it in turns to be the bad guy.

Jacqueline and I shared the same interests. We sang in the choir, and we both learned musical instruments. I played the clarinet; she played the flute. We were innocents – in first year we were still playing with Barbie dolls, and later on, neither of us were interested in the cool crowd who went to the disco.

It didn't seem to matter that we came from such different backgrounds, but we were, now I look back, chalk and cheese. She had the best pencil cases and pens, and I was the poor child, with no pencil case.

Jacqueline lived in a beautiful detached house. An only child, her mummy and daddy adored her. She had a pet cow! I had to queue for my free meal ticket; it felt as if I was begging all the time. It was as if the teacher, Mrs Adair, liked seeing my humiliation. I'd be nearing the front of the line, and she'd roar, 'Sharon! Get to the back of the line.' That kept happening, and went on, until Mum went to the headmaster to complain. She said, 'The teachers here don't like Chinese people.' After that, it stopped.

I wasn't interested in boys as a teenager, but for some reason they were interested in me. When I was fourteen, this boy, Aaron, asked me out. Being an innocent, I naturally said, 'no,' and that infuriated him. He wasn't used to being turned down and retaliated by calling me names. One day, he spat at me. His friends all laughed, as if it was great sport. I've never forgotten the humiliation.

There were two especially good-looking boys at school, Spud and Gibby. Everyone loved them! One day, the girls in my class asked Spud, 'who is the nicest girl in the class?' I'm pretty sure they expected him to choose Sonia, because she worked her way between them. If she wasn't going out with one of them, she'd be going out with the other. So, when he said, 'Sharon Truesdale,' they weren't too pleased. And that's when my real problems started.

These girls had never noticed me before, since I was far from cool, but now they decided they disliked me. They started calling me names and calling my mum names. They'd wait for me after school, and shout out, 'There goes Chinky.' I see now that they were jealous, but their bitchiness really affected me. It made me more determined than ever to avoid boys.

Of course, that didn't last! At fifteen, when Geoff, a boy a few years older than me took an interest, and asked me out, I agreed, and was happy to. We were together for four years – we even got engaged! But when I set off to study law, he couldn't cope with the long-distance relationship. He stopped contacting me, and I heard he had found someone else.

That hit me hard. Was my mum, right? Were all men bastards who just used you for sex? I got over my bitterness because my mantra for life has always been to forgive, forget, and get on with my life. Geoff and I have remained friends to this day.

It had taken me a while to realise that whilst my childhood had been difficult, James's was even more troubled. Yes, it was more prosperous than mine – and his dad was in his life - but it takes love to nurture a child, and whilst there was not a lot of love in my family, there was rather less in his.

But by the time James and I moved in with his mother, it was, essentially, a happy house. Joyce had married again, and her two sons with Davy were fun to have around the place. But damage, once done, doesn't easily lift. And if Joyce had learned that women should be subservient, and that accepting a black eye here and there was par for the course, James had witnessed all that too.

Strength and dominance were part of being a man. That's what he'd learned. And if James had charm too – and he had – bucket loads of it – I was starting to realise that there was another side to him. And that was altogether darker.

After three, long, months of living with his family we found a house. I was thrilled! This was the new start I had longed for. And when the line on a pregnancy test went blue, and I told James the news, we were both over the moon! He was so proud. This was proof of his manhood. Away from his family home, his mood calmed too, and I was filled with hope.

2

Young Matthew

'I wish I was dead.'

'What did you say?' Catching seven-year-old Matthew by the shoulders, I turned him to face me, looking into the eyes that were so like my own.

He pulled away, and muttered under his breath, so that I had to strain to hear him.

'I'm going to kill myself with a knife.'

My heart nearly stopped with the shock of it. Yet his pronouncement didn't come completely out of the blue. Matthew's problems started early. You could say they began before he'd even been born. In early pregnancy, I had started to bleed. Fearing the worst, I went to my doctor, and he sent me on to hospital. The technician, scanning me, couldn't find any sign of a baby. 'I don't think you're pregnant,' she said. 'Could you have made a mistake?'

She called in a doctor who took some blood, and, having tested it, said, 'You *are* pregnant. You weren't wrong about that; but it's an ectopic pregnancy.'

I'd never heard of that. 'What does it mean?'

'The baby is growing in your fallopian tube.'

I frowned, trying to take it in.

'I'm really sorry.'

'But what does that mean?'

'We'll have to remove it.'

I cried then, and I cried again when I came around after the operation. James visited, and he was nice. He said not to worry, that we could just try again. Joyce wasn't so sympathetic. 'Poor James,' she said, ignoring the tears I was now trying hard to hide.

'Poor James?'

'He was so looking forwards to be a dad.'

'Well, yes. And I was pretty keen to be a mum, too.' Did she blame me for losing the baby? For somehow being bad breeding material?

'If you hadn't told everyone you were pregnant so early on, this would never have happened.'

Back at home, I kept crying. I couldn't stop. I vomited too. 'It's bizarre,' I said. 'I feel like I've got morning sickness, but I'm not even pregnant. I don't understand it.'

I went back to my doctor.

'It'll be the anaesthetic,' he said. 'Give it a few days and I'm sure you'll be fine.'

I did, and I wasn't. I went back again, and another test showed that I was still pregnant. That made the doctor scratch his head. 'It must've been twins,' he said. 'And you lost one.'

The sickness dogged me for a while. I didn't feel like going out, but once it passed, we decided to go to Dublin for a weekend. James's friends, Gary and Grainne came too. On the way, we stopped for petrol. James sat in the driver's seat, whilst Gary filled the tank. Afterwards, he jumped back into the car, slammed the door, and James sped off. 'What's that about?' I said. 'You haven't paid?'

The other three laughed and my heart sank. It was a terrible weekend, because I realised, as never before, that James was not the person I'd thought. I don't drink, and the three of them were tanked up for most of the weekend. 'You're just a killjoy,' James said when I complained. And, when, driving like a maniac, he scared the living daylights out of me, I muttered that I hated him, and wouldn't want him around my baby.

Pushing down the accelerator, his knuckles turned white. And he said, 'Take that back. If you ever think of leaving me, I'll kill the two of us.'

I screamed at him to slow down, and thankfully he did. And after that, things calmed down a little.

The sickness cleared, and at six months pregnant I felt good. We were both looking forwards to the birth, anxious to be a real family. But one morning, jerking awake from a dream, I couldn't breathe, and realised that James's hands were round my neck.

I fought him off. That wasn't easy. James is much stronger than I am, but perhaps all he wanted was a reaction. Well he got that all right. I sat up, gasping for air, and hoped he'd say sorry. But he was shouting at me. 'Where are my jeans? Where did you put them? Tell me now, or I'll be late for work.'

'Aren't they in the hot-press?'

He ran off to look and came back wearing them. 'How was I to know,' he said, instead of saying, 'sorry.'

'James, that's where your clean work clothes go. You know that.'

Why didn't I leave him then? Because I loved him. Because he came home contrite. Because he promised nothing like that would ever happen again. Did I believe him? I wanted to.

And it *didn't* happen again. Not like that. And if he screamed at me each night, and threw his dinner across the room, or shouted and threatened me, that was just his temper. Maybe Joyce was right. Maybe he couldn't help it. And he did, always, say sorry.

The baby was due on April 3rd, 1995. I hoped it wouldn't arrive on April Fool's Day, and as it turned out, that would have been the least of my problems. Towards the end of my pregnancy, the doctor became concerned. 'Your blood pressure is up,' he said. 'We'll have to watch that.' When my urine tested positive for protein, and my ankles and face swelled up, I was admitted to hospital with pre-eclampsia.

I didn't feel too bad; but I looked like Michelin woman from all the swelling. 'Where are you Sharon,' James joked, slumping in the chair beside the bed.

When the doctor announced that I was to be induced, I felt such joy. 'I'll be a mother tonight,' I said. But no such luck. They tried to start me off with pessaries; they tried three times, and eventually contractions started to kick in.

I held Matthew when he was born. I held him close, hoping he would breastfeed, but he seemed too sleepy. I was unwell for a while. I had a haemorrhage and needed a blood transfusion. And the next day Matthew had jaundice and was sleepy and floppy.

It didn't dent anyone's happiness. James had a permanent grin on his face. My mum was over the moon, and my sisters were cock-a-hoop. Joyce already had grandchildren, but on my side, he was the first grandson, the first nephew, the first everything! It was brilliant!

After 10 days we returned home to our estate house. I felt so proud bringing the beautiful Moses-basket into our house in the Newpark estate. I was 21; I was married; and I had my baby, my beautiful little boy.

James was working for a lorry company making trailers at the time, and I worked for three nights a week – leaving Matthew with Mum. She lived just across the road, so this arrangement worked out well. But, taking advantage of this, James started going out with his mates; basically, living the single life.

I didn't mind at first. I had my baby, and reasoned that James needed an evening out with his friends, but then the nights out escalated. There were times when I'd wake in the morning and realise his side of the bed hadn't been slept in. There were nights when I wished he'd stayed out, because he arrived in the small hours blocked, shouting and breaking things.

One evening, I decided to watch a movie. Maria, my sister, said that there was a film coming up on TV, Sleepers, that I would enjoy. 'It will be just your kind of thing,' she said.

I waited, impatiently, until the night it was on, and, expecting James home for dinner, I ordered takeaway beef curry, fried rice, chips and prawn crackers. He wasn't home by 9.00pm, so leaving his share in the oven, I settled down in front of the television.

It was after 10pm when James appeared at the entrance of the living room. The smell of alcohol would have knocked you flat. He stood at the door looking at me, and said, 'I'm going to kill you'

Ignoring him, I said, 'I'm watching this film – the one I told you about.' I hoped this would distract him. But it was if as he hadn't heard me.

'I'm going to kill you' He'd raised his voice now. 'I dreamt about it; I'll do it with a knife.'

There was a dangerous glint in his eye. I thought, oh God, he means it! And from that moment I was wary. And the next time he threatened me he had baby Matthew in his arms – and I feared for him too. That was it! I left him the following day and went across the road to stay with Mum.

It wasn't a difficult decision. I'd watched my mum and dad argue. Mum had stayed out of a sense of misplaced loyalty, only to be unceremoniously dumped when Dad met someone, he considered more appealing. I wasn't going to make the same mistake! I was lucky, and managed to get a housing executive house, so leaving James in the matrimonial home.

I walked out with a nothing but a single bag of belongings, and my baby son. James wasn't pleased. He'd lost control of me, and he ended up damaging the house. My name was on the mortgage, meaning that I was still financially responsible for it. I ended up getting a court order to get him out, so that the house could be sold.

James's response was to clear the whole house. When I went around to check, I couldn't find any sign of baby Matthew's things. His cot, clothes, everything was gone. I told the police, and they contacted his family, and told them that if the things were not returned, James would be arrested. Funny how everything reappeared the next day! James moved on, getting a flat in Newpark, just a road away from Caulside, where Matthew and I now lived.

I was still scared of James – terrified of his temper – but baby Matthew adored his father, and four months later, around the time of Matthew's second birthday, we decided to give our marriage another chance. James asked me out to dinner. We had a lovely time. We really did. All the romance of the early days was back, and I invited James back to the house, where we had a night of passion.

Waking in his arms I felt so happy. It was like all the bad stuff had never happened. Later that day, I stood on the bed reaching into the top of the wardrobe for some clean sheets, and I was singing, feeling carefree for the first time in ages, when James appeared at the bedroom door, Matthew at his feet.

'What are you so happy about,' he said. Then he thumped the door so hard that it broke. Matthew ran from him in terror, holding out his arms to me, so I scooped him up, and said, 'How dare you break up my house.'

He looked at me in astonishment, his mouth open, as if he didn't know this new version of Sharon; this strong confident woman who was well capable of sticking up for herself. He left without saying a word, leaving Matthew screaming, inconsolable.

'That's it,' I shouted to his back. 'We're finished.' And we were. We were, except that, as fate would have it, that night had produced results. I was pregnant again.

I didn't realise it. Not for ages. I went to the doctor with sickness, and he diagnosed flu. 'It's going around,' he said. But then, I started vomiting, and the only time that happens is when I'm pregnant. I went back to the doctor, and, confirming the pregnancy, he looked at me, and shook his head, unsmiling. Knowing what I had been going through the previous year he said, 'If you don't want this baby there are other options.'

What was he saying? That I wanted to get rid of it? I was horrified. 'No, no, this is *my* baby, it's been given to me for a reason.' I didn't say it to him, but I fervently believe that a baby is a gift from God, and I'm so grateful to Him for allowing me to become pregnant so easily.

Yes, James was out of the picture, but that made little difference to my mindset. I liked the idea of both my children having the same father. That felt right. When the pregnancy started to show, James got back in touch, and said, 'Sharon, it's my child. Can I come back?'

Did I want him back? Well, I still loved him, and I really wanted to believe him when he swore how much he had changed. If he had, life would be so good. I wanted us all to be together, but felt, that as a compromise, maybe I should live in my house, he in his. That way, I thought, our relationship had a chance.

'I'll give you one more chance to be a father,' I said. 'But don't think you're getting back to live with me.'

He didn't like that. He wanted all or nothing. But I knew that to him, 'all', meant me tied to the house with the children, and him living a single man's life, visiting when it suited. And there was no way I would agree to that. I no longer trusted him – and besides, there were times I was actually scared of him, so why would I want him in my house?

He was with me when Natasha made her way into the world, on 29th May 1997, but there wasn't the same excitement around her birth. In James's eyes, a second child, and a daughter was never going to be as special. Not to him; not to his family.

James wanted contact with the children – and Joyce helped in this; we arranged for him to see them at her house. The problem was, that he wasn't prepared to give me maintenance for the children's care. He believed that, as I had made the decision to bring the children up alone, none of the financial responsibility lay with him.

When Natasha was a one year old, I claimed benefit as a one parent family, and the social security benefits office asked if James was contributing. I explained that I'd rather manage without his input, but they continued to investigate. He wasn't prepared to hand over money, and, when they discovered that he had cash in hand from working for a builder, he left the country and moved to Jersey.

That was the last I heard of him for the next five years. I kept in touch with Joyce, because I value family and felt this was important. We visited her every month, but with the tacit agreement that James was never mentioned.

And he wasn't. Until he moved back to Northern Ireland, and asked me, through Joyce, if he could see Matthew and Natasha. I dreaded seeing him again, but Joyce said he had changed. And when I set eyes on him, he did seem to have matured. He had a new girlfriend, Tina, who had two children from a previous relationship. Seeing how calm and comfortable they were together, I relaxed. Surely now everything could be different? Tina seemed nice, and I trusted her, so, after a few months – when things were progressing well, I was happy for the children to have contact with their father. The arrangement made me happy, because Matthew needed his father. But over the months, when Matthew was visiting his father, my lovely innocent boy was gradually changing.

One day, I was doing the washing up, when I felt a thump on my back. Matthew was standing there. He said, 'Mummy, you're a whore.'

'What did you say?'

'You're a whore.'

'Do you know what that means?'

He shook his head. 'No. But Daddy told me. He says so.'

That was unsettling, but it wasn't the worst of it. There were times, after that, that Matthew would come home crying, and then he started wetting the bed. He wouldn't say what was wrong. It was weird. Because when I asked him what he had done with James, he seemed enthusiastic.

'Boxing!' he'd say. 'It was ace!'

I didn't like the idea of that, but I remembered James telling me that his dad had taught him to box, to toughen him up. I let it go.

When Matthew came home with bruises on his chest, and a Chinese burn on his head, I'd had enough. When I asked Matthew what had happened, he said his dad had been wrestling him.

That was it. I stopped contact. And it wasn't just the wrestling. Matthew's behaviour had become increasingly erratic. He'd come home crying, and would scratch his face and bang his head, repeatedly against the wall. When I tried to contain him, and to find out what was wrong, he turned on me. He kicked out and hit me. One time he came at me with a belt. It was both bizarre and horrifying.

Furious that he wasn't allowed to see his children, James took me to court - to the Ballymena Family Court. When the judge asked him how Matthew had got his bruises, he said, 'Well you know the way you hold a child down, and you put a trainer on his head, and twist it like this?'

The court descended into silence. 'I'm sorry?' said the judge. 'Could you say that to me again.'

James did, and the case was thrown out of court. The judge said there was no way James would be allowed to see Matthew and Natasha. James appealed on a legal point. In fact, there were two points for appeal; one where he again challenged contact, and the other concerning their names.

I had reverted to my maiden name, and had been using it, also, for the children. James didn't like this and wanted them known as Thompson. He employed a barrister through Legal

Aid, but since I was working, I was ineligible, and, unwilling to fork out more money, having recently paid for my divorce, decided to represent myself, with the support of my sister, Maria.

Asked when the children's birthdays were, on the stand, James didn't know. Then James's barrister questioned whether, Natasha was his daughter.

'She is,' I said, 'but if James doesn't think she is, I will be happy for her to be taken off the proceedings.'

She immediately moved on to other matters. We discussed the toy gun James had bought Matthew for Christmas. He knew that I didn't like what guns represented.

'I think it was a hidden message to me,' I said, explaining how James had used his fingers as a gun as he role-played shooting me.

Asked, again, about the Chinese burn, he changed his story, but then he lost his temper, and said, 'If my wife can come up to the stand, I'll show the court a Chinese burn.'

Summing up, the Judge stated that as parents, James and I clearly had different standards. 'I suggest Mr Thompson should do a parenting course with the NSPCC,' he said. The course was arranged, but James consistently failed to turn up.

As for the name issue, James eventually withdrew his application, and I had the children's names legally changed to Truesdale.

They talk of the innocence of children; of how precious childhood is, but Matthew lost his innocence so early. I hoped that he didn't remember the broken door – or the time a brick came flying through the kitchen window, causing glass to shower round the room, and cut the toddler's feet. And though he had a scar from that, which was exacerbated when James stamped on him, I imagine he was too young for the specifics to stay with him, but spending unsupervised time? That was a different story.

Matthew's behaviour became so untruly, it ruined our Christmas in 2001. In March, I asked for help. My mother offered to look after her grandson. When she was also unable to control him, she carted him off to the GP and he went to CAMHS- an organisation I would come to know only too well.

Worried, I stopped all contact, and like magic, the trouble ceased. I breathed a big sigh of relief.

3

The Trouble Begins

I've always had an instinctive desire to keep my children safe; and I was aware that James wasn't the only source of potential trouble. Conflict in Northern Ireland was officially over – the Good Friday agreement was signed when Matthew was just three years old – but there were still dissident groups around, and I was determined to shelter my children.

When they were young, Matthew and Natasha didn't even realise that there were religious differences. They had friends from all walks of life, and that is the way I liked it. On 12th July, when, every year, the Orangemen's march causes civil unrest, Matthew saw all the Union Jacks and smiled in excitement.

'Look Mum,' he said, pointing through the car window. 'Look at all the flags. Is it the circus? Can we go?'

'Please!' said Natasha, craning her neck to look out of the window.

I talked my way out of that one, and sighed relief, but then, the children focused on all the bonfires. They begged to be allowed to join the fun.

Matthew left the playschool where his grandmother, Joyce, worked when he was four years old and ready to move to Primary School. We chose the one my brother had attended because he had been happy there, and Matthew settled down well. He liked school.

I do remember one untoward incident. There was a boy, Dillon, who bullied Matthew. He could cope with the name calling; he ignored it, but when Dillon invited the whole class to his birthday party – except for Matthew, that really hurt him. I was appalled. How can children be so cruel, and how can their parents allow it? I spoke to the school, but there was little support.

Meanwhile, my life was going well. I met a lovely man, Mark, at a local night club, and when Matthew was nine, our daughter, Annie Jean was born. Although we both love her to bits, the relationship between us didn't work out long term, and we've split, but we've remained good friends and have happily co-parented her ever since.

Matthew was bright. But when, at eleven, he moved on to Cambridge House Grammar School, his problems really started. Reaching home each day, he seemed subdued. He denied that there was anything wrong, and I hoped it was just my imagination. But when, in the summer, we went shopping for a new uniform, my suspicions were confirmed. Trying on his new shoes – big size two - he grinned at me. I tousled his hair, but he pulled away.

'I'm bigger now.'

'You are.'

He looked up, and flashed me his irresistible, slightly lopsided grin. 'Sure, I'll not get bullied.'

That remark threw me. But I didn't say anything right away. I waited until we got home to question him. 'Matthew, were you bullied last year?' I asked.

He nodded. 'They call me chinky,' he said, close to tears.

'That's tough,' I said.

'And they throw my schoolbag around. And take things.' His head down, he was muttering, making it difficult for me to catch his words.

Pulling him towards, me, I hugged him, cross with myself for not picking up the signs earlier. Because, now I thought about it, the signs had been there. It all made sense. Sense of the times Matthew had 'lost' his Nike trainers and needed money for another pair. Or the time he couldn't find his whole PE Kit. I'd been so angry with him for that and had asked him if he thought I was made of money.

'Why didn't you tell me,' I asked, feeling ashamed.

He shrugged.

'Promise me, Matthew, you won't keep anything from me again. If you don't tell me these things, I can't help you.'

He said he would be more open, but as it turned out, I couldn't help him anyway. I tried, but my input didn't help Matthew at all. In fact, it had the opposite effect.

Natasha was still at Antrim Primary School at the time, but she and Matthew hatched a plot to get my views on smoking. Natasha opened the discussion. Arriving in from school one day, she said, 'What would you do if one of your children was smoking?'

Realising at once that she meant Matthew, and that he *was* smoking, I kept calm, and explained that smoking is not good for you. I told them all about lung cancer and related illnesses, but knowing that teenagers think they're immortal, I was alarmed, and went into the school to voice my suspicions. My concerns were brushed aside.

'There are no children smoking here,' I was told. 'We have a no smoking policy.'

'Is that so?' I said. 'Then how come, when I drive past the school, I see children smoking on the football pitch?'

It was the worst thing I could have done. The school took action against the smokers, and policed the grounds regularly, and, somehow, Matthew's involvement in that became known. The bullying increased, and it didn't only come from the pupils. Matthew was picked on by the teachers too. If the whole class performed a misdemeanour – say everyone was using their mobile phone in class, Matthew would be the one in trouble.

One day I was hauled into school, to see the principle. She handed me a penknife – a souvenir Matthew had brought back from our holidays to use when he went fishing.

'Matthew brought this into school, and threatened another pupil,' she said.

That didn't sound like Matthew. And when I asked him about it, he said he had simply been showing the knife to one of the girls. Anyway, I mentioned to the principle that Matthew was being bullied, and, referring to the bullying policy, she denied it. The school never admitted, officially, that there was a problem. But one day in October, when I was in the school, a teacher stopped me in the corridor and said, 'It's awful what Matthew is experiencing from those boys, but don't worry. The troublemakers are leaving in February.'

I asked what she was talking about. And she mentioned two boys, sons of paramilitaries, who were causing havoc in the school. My fears confirmed, I now felt able to talk to Matthew about it. He was happy to talk. We've always had a good relationship, and I asked him why he'd not felt able to confide in me before. He explained that to do so would make him a tout – and that would have got him into more trouble. But now that the teacher was the tout, he was free to talk. Nothing changed though. And I realised that the principal was afraid to confront the bullies because of their paramilitary connections.

Matthew was seeing a school counsellor, Anne, at the time – someone whose advice he listened to and trusted. And she felt it would be in his best interests to change schools – he was in fourth year at the time. She helped him get a transfer to a school in Antrim. Whilst I was happy with that, it saddened me that the school had not given us support.

Matthew wasn't the only student that I knew of to suffer taunts. The two boys started to bully his friend Aaron, too. And mainly, it seems, because his mother was from Pakistan. Both boys got threatened and pulled into fights. Bullying wasn't new to the school; it had been local news that a young boy had completed suicide from bullying, yet the school clearly hadn't learned from this.

With the transfer, it seemed that Matthew's troubles were over. He was happy! At least, he was happy for the first few months at Parkhall. So, when he came home with a black eye, I was shocked. The bullying had started again! I was in despair, but that's when a kind of miracle happened. His cousin, on his father's side, Stuart - the son of Gary and Eleanor who came to my wedding - also attended the school. They took Matthew under their wing, and life looked up. They were well liked, and a little feared, and Matthew blossomed.

When he asked if he could get in touch with his dad again, I hesitated, remembering all that had gone on when Matthew was younger. I spoke to my solicitor, and then to a social worker. She said that, in practical terms, Matthew was no longer under my control. 'It would be easy enough for him to jump onto a bus and go and find his dad,' she said. 'And now that he has become friends with his cousins, he could easily have contact with his dad – and you wouldn't know anything about it.'

She said that if I wanted to keep a good relationship with Matthew, I had to be seen to support his decision, even if I believed this would not be good for him. I still had my doubts, but eventually I agreed. James seemed settled now that he was happy with Tina. They'd had a baby together. Jay was now six years old. I thought the contact would do Matthew good, and at first, it did. James seemed to love getting to know his teenage son. He offered Matthew a room in the house, and, at Christmas, he showered him with presents.

Matthew proudly showed off his new designer jeans, and after-shave. And if they were the first presents he had received from his father in five years, well, it was better than nothing.

When Matthew asked if he could move in with his dad, though, I felt hurt. More than that, I was heartbroken. But after all the talks we'd had over the years; all the negotiations over half-term breaks, I felt unable to refuse him. And if the look of triumph on James's face irked me, and his promises to give Matthew a converted room and a motorbike seemed excessive, I swallowed my objections and hoped for the best. Maybe James was being sincere when he said, 'Matthew can see you anytime.' And if he enjoyed adding, 'I know what it's like not to have access to your kids,' I managed not to rise to the bait.

This meant a change of school and a whole new uniform, but I waved him off, first making him promise to visit often. And as it turned out, there wasn't time for that. I hadn't lost my son – or not for long. A week after he had moved out, I opened the door to find him on the doorstep looking cowed.

'Hello, stranger,' I said. 'What's up?'

Matthew stomped in, threw his rucksack down, slumped onto the sofa and turned on the TV. 'Dad's the worst,' he said. It turned out that his dad had given him a hiding. 'And I didn't do anything wrong,'

I asked him to tell me exactly what had happened.

'Dad punched me in the face.'

'Ok,' I said, swallowing. 'Can you tell me why?'

'I asked to come home, because I don't like Carrickfergus Secondary School.' He looked at me, shyly. 'And I told him I missed you, Ma.'

I wasn't surprised by this development, and was, of course, delighted to have my son home again, but I was aware that Matthew was disappointed that the arrangement hadn't worked. Clearly, he felt let down. And when he continued to see the cousins that James had introduced him to, meeting up with them in Carrickfergus, I was pleased for him. I knew that, much as he loved his sisters and me, we couldn't provide the same camaraderie that his, male, cousins could.

They weren't always the best of influence. One evening, they were all drinking in a carpark, when James walked by. He pretended he hadn't seen them, but Matthew shouted at him, and Tina called the police to arrest them. The incident caused a huge rift between father and son. I was angry with Matthew, but sad, too. All he ever wanted was to be accepted and loved by his father.

I gave him hell over the drinking, and Matthew promised it wouldn't happen again. And when, on a midweek evening, he asked if he could go to his friend, Jordan's house, and play on his X box, I didn't see any harm in it, and agreed. How was I to know that it was the lad's mother's 30th birthday, and that she would buy her son a bottle of vodka? Or that they would drink it, then wander, drunk, around the estate?

Who would have guessed that they would end up in someone's garage or that they would 'lift' a rucksack full of crisps and chocolate? They almost got away with it. They were back at Jordan's house, finishing that game on the X Box, when the police caught up with them, arresting them for breaking into the garage.

Something broke in Matthew after that, and he started leaving school early and experimenting with cannabis. With this addiction came the costs. From then on, he was in and out of court time and time again for shoplifting, mostly when he was off his head and needing munchies. He never even remembered what he had done.

There wasn't any badness in Matthew. The problem was that he wanted to please people. He was loved by everybody, and, particularly after being bullied, he wanted it to stay that way. He did all kinds of good deeds. He painted his nana's house, helped with my shopping, cooked for me, and told constant jokes to keep me amused.

The problem was, that he didn't always differentiate the things that were helpful, and those that were damaging. If one of his friends said, 'Smoke a joint,' or 'play a game of football,' he would.

And of course, once he got used to that illegal high – mainly from cannabis – he needed money to fund his habit. And from the ages of 13 to 15, he was in and out of court. His reputation in the town was well known, and as a consequence, everybody knew me too.

Worried though I was, for Matthew, I was pleased when he attended court. He had to know his actions carried consequences. And when, one time, he was in court for an offence carried out around alcohol, whilst his friend and co-conspirator was given a small fine, Matthew was remanded at Woodlands. I was *not* pleased. I was starting to see that the justice system, which I had always assumed was fair, was far from it. It seemed that it was a performance, and whoever put on the best show won. What sort of a message was that for a lad in trouble?

I was starting to see inequalities in how people are treated. I often wondered would it make a difference if the judge sitting there, dishing out sentences, knew that the young boy in front of him was the same young boy he had protected all those years before from his violent father?

By this time, my current partner, Terry had entered my life. We met in 2009, when Matthew was 15, and he proved a good influence on my son. Altogether, life seemed to be settling down, but then another complication entered Matthew's life, in the form of a girl called Shanice.

When I first saw Shanice, in 2010, I could understand, at once, what Matthew saw in her. At 17, she was older than he was, and she was beautiful. She was slim, with a sheath of shiny blonde hair, and she looked after herself. I never saw her without makeup, and she was always well groomed.

Matthew had another girlfriend at the time, and she said she had a boyfriend, so, at first, I saw no harm in the friendship, but when, a few months later, Matthew told me the two of them were now an item, I was worried. But Shanice seemed to be a good influence. Done with partying, she had moved out of her troubled home to live with her grandmother; and now seemed happy to be at home watching DVD's. I relaxed, happy that he had found her. They became inseparable, and all Matthew wanted was to stay home with Shanice. Off the streets, he was safe and would keep out of trouble. I decided she was an angel!

'I love Shanice,' said Annie Jean, and the older girl was the perfect big sister, painting Annie-Jean's nails for her, and helping Natasha do her hair. She was the perfect surrogate daughter too. Not to mention the perfect girlfriend for Matthew. I couldn't have been happier.

In the end, the age gap proved a problem. Three years mightn't seem much, but there was a yawning difference between 15 and 18 – not to mention in Matthew and Shanice's experience. Shanice worked, in the play area of Adventure Island, on shifts, and so she had money, whereas Matthew, very often didn't.

'Do you realise Matthew only has pocket money, and sometimes not even that?' I asked her once.

More serious than that, though, Shanice wanted a baby. Her sister became pregnant at 16, to a boy a year younger, and Shanice felt left out. I had a word with her, saying that a baby would disrupt both her and Matthew's future – that they were too young, but she didn't listen. And when, in January, in the same week that I discovered that I was pregnant, with my partner Terry's baby, she announced that she was pregnant too.

Shanice was excited – and pictured herself moving in with me. I told her that was impossible, and that she would have to sort herself out, and continue to live with her granny, and she accepted that. But a week before her nephew was born, Shanice suffered a miscarriage. And following that, and the birth of my baby, Daniel, on 25th June, her relationship with Matthew deteriorated. They had terrible, vicious rows.

Matthew was thrilled when his dad asked him to his 40th birthday party, and Shanice tagged along with him. But she ignored Matthew and spent the night flirting with his cousin, Stuart. Their relationship went from bad to worse; Matthew was finding it hard to cope with her, and in the end, I barred her from the house.

In September 2011, Matthew had started at the Oriel Training, hoping to become a chef like my brother, Richard. His placement was in the Dunadry Hotel. Shortly after starting there, he met another girl, Bronagh, and they started going out together. I was pleased. Things were looking up for Matthew; he was behaving like a normal 16-year-old.

I relaxed for a while, happy that Shanice was out of the picture, but that scenario wasn't to last. Shanice accused Matthew of rape – a charge he strenuously denied – but he was dragged through the courts causing him extreme distress, before, finally, Shanice admitted that it wasn't true. In October 2011, she went into the Antrim police station to withdraw the charges against him.

He expected his ongoing legal case to be resolved, but the PPS said they still wanted to proceed, and by November, he was back in court. The case dragged on. It was changed to the County Court, and there were several adjournments before it was finally dismissed, the following May. By this stage Matthew's mental health had deteriorated, and his relationship with Bronagh had cooled.

'We're two different people, with different interests,' he told me. 'We've agreed to go our separate ways.'

When the PSNI asked me If I wanted to prosecute Shanice for having sex with an underage boy, I was aghast. She needed support, not a police record. And you would think that enough time had already been wasted on the case, what with all the toing and froing. Wasn't it all a waste of taxpayer's money? I was struck, once again, by the inadequacies of a legal system which fails to provide justice for everyone.

But why *had* she lied? Later, it transpired that she wanted money so that she and Matthew could buy a house. She'd reasoned that if Matthew pleaded guilty, she could get compensation, and that my insurance would pay. Hadn't she realised the possible consequences of such foolishness?

The main consequence had been the level of Matthew's distress. He loved Shanice and could not understand why she seemed set to destroy him. Every time a solicitor's letter arrived, or Matthew had to visit the police station, his level of self-harm would increase. I watched with horror and bemusement. It's hard to observe your son's terror with the criminal justice system, particularly when he is so in love, he would risk anything to please his girlfriend. When I read the research showing that first love can be a powerful addiction, I could only nod my head in recognition. No question, Matthew was addicted to Shanice.

4

Nearing the End

When, in January 2019, taking some clean clothes into Matthew's room, I found him with my dressing-gown cord round his neck, I was profoundly shocked. What mother wouldn't be? Yet part of me understood that the strain of the court case, hanging over him like a dead weight had become simply too much to bear.

When, some while later, he attempted an overdose I knew I had to intervene. I fixed for an emergency appointment with doctors. He told the doctor that he was unable to sleep, and in fact hadn't slept for some time. The doctor asked how he could help, and Matthew said, 'Give me a lethal injection so I can die.'

Was it *my* fault? Had I not supported him enough? I tried to dismiss that thought and went all out to help him. I knew the drill through my job in youth work. I've completed ASIST Training and MHFA Training, so I knew what to do in the situation. And yet, I began to doubt myself.

But if I doubted myself, I couldn't fault Terry. He also worked in the Youth Service, and he was especially helpful. His job, at that time, was working in a project supporting young men with mental health problems. We both had a good understanding of how to signpost and help marginalised and 'at risk,' young people.

The skills needed to connect and engage with young people and adults, was helpful when it came to deal with our families. Matthew confided in me, always, and I challenged, educated and supported him the best way I could; both as a mother, and by seeking other services when necessary.

It's partly my training; partly my personality. Once, when I was shopping in Primark, minding my own business, a stranger approached me and related her whole life story. And that's not the only time it's happened; people randomly confide in me. They perhaps sense that I'm approachable. I care, and I will listen.

I remember the first time that Matthew took tablets – enough to give him a sore head – not, thankfully enough to kill himself, he told me how disappointed he had been to wake up and find himself alive. When Terry came back from work, I asked Matthew to repeat what he had said to me. 'Tell Terry why you're not feeling well,' I said.

'I took an overdose,' said Matthew.

Terry asked why. He listened, as Matthew listed his woes. Then he sighed. Sitting on the sofa, asking Matthew to sit down beside him, he said, 'I've had a pretty bad day at work today. I've come from a community that is devastated. Do you want to know why?'

Matthew grunted in reply.

'A young boy has taken his own life.'

Matthew shrugged. 'Sure, everyone will be sad for a week or two. But they'll get over it. It'll be alright.'

Looking Matthew in the eye, Terry asked him how long it had been since he'd fallen out with his former girlfriend, Shanice.

'A year I suppose. Well, off and on.'

'Are you still missing her?'

Matthew nodded.

'Well, how do you think your mum would feel if something happened to you. Her son?'

He looked at me. Then he looked away. Had he taken that in? Or did he still believe that my life would continue as before.

Grateful as I was to Terry, I didn't feel entirely reassured. I couldn't just leave it at that. I decided to talk to Matthew's friends about the attempt.

'Oh Ma!' said Matthew, when I mentioned what I planned. But he didn't say I shouldn't tell them. I think, deep down, that he wanted them to know.

They listened but had trouble believing me.

'Matthew?'

'Yeah.'

'But he's always happy. He's the life and soul.'

And maybe that was the problem. He didn't show his feelings. Not to them.

I told his father, James, too. I wasn't leaving anything to chance. I said, 'Matthew's not feeling too good.' And he popped around occasionally, threw him a packet of cigarettes, and left, muttering, 'I love you, son.'

We made the house safe, hiding tablets. My mother took out a gym membership for Matthew. He was enthusiastic, taking his fitness seriously. He was constantly out with his friends. But there were times, when something happened, or the court case threatened to blow, that he would flip into uncontrollable anger and rage – rage that he targeted at himself and would cause self-harm. He would cut himself or bang his head off the walls. He would have a joint in order to dull the pain, but it only made his mood worse. I lived in dread of those very worst times, when he made those attempts to take his life. It was like living on a knife edge.

Five months before Matthew died, I persuaded him to go to CAMHS – The Child and Adolescent Mental Health Service. He had been referred to them on several previous occasions, and if anyone could help him, I thought, they could. But they let us down. They let Matthew down. Lying there, that night, remembering how they had responded to him, I inwardly seethed.

Matthew hadn't wanted to go. He hated anything to do with the mental health services. I pleaded with him, and then, feeling frightened, I started to cry in despair. 'I'm frightened Matthew', I said. 'I need help in order to help you, and if you want to live, you need help. Don't you see?' I became hysterical. 'The way you're feeling, Matthew, it's just not right.'

Finally, Matthew agreed. He would accompany me there. 'But only to keep you quiet,' he said, raising his eyebrows.

I sighed my relief and led him out to the car. We were both quiet in the waiting room, but I was full of hope. Surely Matthew would now receive the help he so badly needed? We were called in.

There were three people waiting for us, in that room; a psychiatrist, a counsellor and a social worker. They asked Matthew how he was, and he told the truth. He talked of his low mood and admitted to self-harm. Then he looked at me for support, and when I related everything that had happened at home. Matthew nodded his agreement.

'Yes,' he said. 'It's like my ma says. I get frustrated with things. I can't help getting angry.'

'And what happens then?'

He repeated that he cut himself. 'Or I throw things. Or hit my head off the wall. I do try,' he said. 'I want to put things right, but something always happens. Something I can't control.' He shrugged. 'Life's just not worth living.'

I took over again then, explaining all that happened, about Shanice, about the court case, and of his precarious relationship with his father. The psychiatrist was busy scribbling notes – notes I later requested.

'April took 2 strips of anti-depressants. Planned, disappointed wasn't successful'

'pulled dressing gown cord around his neck – mum couldn't release it'

'cut himself with knife on neck and arm'

'don't care about anything in general'

'don't think about nothing'

'unclear what would help'

'agreed mum's description is correct'

'mum worried about mood'

'Matthew at GP when asked what would help, he responded, 'lethal injection''

Surely, that list should show them that my concerns for Matthew were justified. That, having tried to end his life, he would, eventually be successful?

I waited for them to take action, as my GP had inferred that they would. Perhaps they would admit him to a psychiatric unit for counselling; or failing that, put him on anti-depressant medication. They didn't. Instead, prescribing Melatonin to help him sleep, they stated that he had no significant mental health issues, and they discharged him from the service.

I couldn't believe it. That decision gave Matthew the impression that his behaviour was completely normal; that all teenagers went through similar issues, and, after all my efforts to get him there, that was the last thing we needed. Matthew hated the term, 'mental health,' and not wanting the stigma attached to himself, had missed appointments in the past. It had taken all my power to get him to this appointment; and it was if they were agreeing with him. I protested. I said again that I felt he was in danger, but they wouldn't listen.

'You're a youth worker,' they said as we got up to leave. 'I suggest you put him on an anger management programme. You have more resources to help your son than we do.' Those words have haunted me.

Did they not realise that it takes an outsider to sort these things out? Leaving, I felt frustrated. I had done my best to keep Matthew safe, but I hadn't been heard. I knew they had done wrong by us. They didn't do what they needed to or what their webpage or leaflets said they would do 'offer support and help to those self-harming or attempting suicide'.

I wanted to challenge them further. I wish now that I had. Why did I not make a complaint, and take Matthew somewhere else? I had phoned Lifeline who told me I was doing all the right things and to give their number to Matthew should he wish to speak to someone. I took him to the GP where he asked for a lethal injection. Did I fail him by not taking him somewhere else like Zest, or Action Mental Health?

Climbing into the car that day, Matthew turned to me and said, 'I told you I was ok.'

Smiling, grimly, I didn't know how to answer.

I relayed all this to Terry. 'They normalised his behaviour,' I said. 'They didn't acknowledge that it was unsafe, and that Matthew, and I, desperately need help.' I sighed. 'They seemed to be implying that Matthew would get better in time, and the trouble is, he seems to believe it too.'

Terry stared at me in disbelief. 'And, obviously, you don't agree?'

'Well, no. How can he improve if CAMHS aren't prepared to give him intervention?'

'Yes, you're right,' said Terry, stroking his chin.

We talked to Matthew, and worked out ways to help him, and things did improve, for a while. Working in a second-hand furniture shop, Darren's Den, Matthew seemed to relish his visits to the gym. If he was taking his health seriously, surely his mind was now on living? He took driving lessons, and his mood lifted.

He was out a lot, the life and soul of the party; a real Romeo with the girls. Always surrounded by friends, the centre of attention he seemed happy. We were close; I could tell when he was masking his sadness, and he had, surely *was* happy.

I didn't relax. I couldn't, because I knew, from experience, that his emotions were on a roller-coaster, and what goes up, must surely come down. I waited, in trepidation, for the next dip. How could I make it less scary not just for Matthew, but for the girls, and for me?

In July, Bronagh phoned and dropped a bombshell. 'I'm pregnant,' she said.

Matthew agreed to provide for the baby but said he didn't want to get back with her. What he *didn't* say, to me, or to Bronagh, was that he was thinking of getting back with Shanice. He was aware that Shanice was bad for him, that the two had an explosive relationship; but his attraction to her was stronger than any drug.

He was good to Bronagh. He accompanied her to the scans, but as the pregnancy progressed, she wanted more. 'She's said, again, that she wants us to get back together,' said Matthew. 'Or as she says, 'she wants the father of her child with her.''

'And what do you want?'

He shrugged. 'I want to see the baby, but I don't want us to get back together.'
He didn't tell me that to be true to his heart he *had* to be with Shanice, and at the time, I didn't know it.

Meanwhile, I felt, inside myself, that something wasn't right. I remember driving along towards Belfast, when I was overcome with a sense of death. It was such a strong sensation that I shared it with the kids.

'If something happens to me, there's a wicker basket in the cupboard in my bedroom', I said. 'I keep all the important paperwork there. Things like passports, birth certificates, all that sort of thing.'

'Mum!' Natasha laughed. 'You're not even forty! Why are you telling us that?'

I shrugged. 'I've just a sense of death,' I said.

Nobody took me seriously. In fact, the wicker basket became a bit of a family joke.

'You can laugh,' I said, 'but you need to know these things. My will is in there too.'

Not even Terry took my fears seriously. 'Your will' he said, rubbing his hands together in mock glee. 'What are you leaving me, then?'

As for Matthew, he said if I was going to die, could I please do it soon. 'I'm a bit broke right now,' he said. 'I could do with a bequest.'

'Very funny!'

Did it occur to me that the death might not be mine? That Matthew might successfully complete suicide? I think not. The thought was simply too horrendous, and, whilst doing everything I could to help Matthew, I pushed it from my mind.

5

The Last Night

I was feeling such a sense of hope. Matthew's mood was good; it had continued to improve since the early summer. And although he and Bronagh hadn't got together again, they had largely resolved their difficulties. And when, on 10th October 2012, she came over to the house, I felt that his life had taken on some normality. All seemed well.

Bronagh came over to our house to talk about the baby, and of Matthew's part in it, after its birth. He was now pleased at the prospect of being a father and was determined to take his role seriously. And, as his job was steady, that seemed a real possibility.

I sat with them, delighted that they were on such friendly terms. I was happy for them both. After all the problems of the past year Matthew was physically fit and mentally stable. Life was good!

At 10.0'clock, wishing them goodnight, I went upstairs to work. I'd recently completed my Masters in Community Youth Work, and had started my dream job, supporting young people with behaviour problems within Special Education, and I had some paperwork to catch up on.

When I left, all was calm. The two of them were flicking through the DVD's to find one to watch. But no sooner had I sat down and turned on my computer, then I heard a piercing scream. I ran downstairs, to find Matthew kneeling beside his bed, his head in his hands, crying.

'What's the matter? Where's Bronagh?' He was in a terrible state.

'Bronagh's gone.'

'Gone? Where? Why?'

'She answered my phone,' he said, staring at his mobile, nestled in his palm. 'Why would *anyone* answer someone else's phone?'

I shrugged.

'I went to the toilet. I'd been gone two minutes, and when I came back, she hit me.' His voice was distorted with tears.

I said just one word. 'Shanice?'

He nodded.

Would that girl ever stop causing my son problems? Wasn't it enough that she accused him of rape, and dragged him through the courts before admitting that she'd been lying all along? Not enough that she'd dated his friends, and his cousins; not to mention having a baby of her own. Would my son continue to be bewitched by her; however, she chose to treat him? Did she enjoy the power?

It seemed that way. Even though they had long since broken up, apparently for good, Shanice seemed incapable of leaving Matthew alone. I don't know what she had said to Bronagh on the phone, but whatever it was, the other girl was not happy. 'Bronagh's only effing calling the police,' said Matthew, visibly shaking. He was terrified of the police. He always had been.

'Will you ring her back? Will you ring Shanice?' He handed me the phone.

'Me? Ring Shanice?'

He nodded. 'She might listen to you. Could you tell her to stop contacting me? It's doing my head in.'

I saw his point. I thought back to that time when I'd first met Shanice; when I thought she would be really good for Matthew. I wondered how it was that she had this strange hold over him. Shanice didn't want Matthew. That was clear. But it appeared that she was damned if anyone else could have him. Shanice knew my thoughts on the matter. And I really did not see how a phone call from me would help the situation

'Matthew,' I said, handing the phone back to him. 'Enough is enough. I think it's time to get an order from a solicitor to tell her to leave you alone.'

He nodded. Then he flung his phone across the room, as if he was bowling it with the intention of knocking out a cricketer. Hitting the wall, it smashed, and fell to the floor in pieces.

He slumped, and dropped to his bed, as if, in breaking his phone, he had released all the tension from his body. It was like watching a balloon deflate. Looking at me, shrugging, he said, 'Why do I bother?'

I couldn't answer him.

'I do try, Mum.'

'I know you do.'

'What more can I do?'

The doorbell rang. Matthew looked at me with scared eyes. 'Will you get it, Ma?'

I nodded, and left, leaving Matthew pacing the room. And there she was, Bronagh, standing on the doorstep, arms crossed, protectively, across her chest. She was calm, but there were tears in her eyes. 'I won't be taken for a fool,' she said.

'Of course not, love.' She came in, making for Matthew's room, and, following her, I sat down beside her. 'Are you all right now, or would you like me to run you home?'

'I'm fine. I'll stay here if that's ok.' She moved away from me and pulled Matthew down beside her.

She said that she hadn't called the police – that it was only a bluff, when the doorbell rang again. Matthew jumped up, looking for all the world like a frightened rabbit. Instead of answering the door, he ran up the stairs. I thought he was overreacting and was surprised to see two burly policemen on the doorstep. 'Can we come in?'

I nodded and stared hard at Bronagh. Following my gaze, the policeman said, 'Was it you who called 999?'

Her face went white. 'I hung up,' she said. 'I didn't speak to anyone.'

The larger man nodded. 'But you *did* dial 999?'

She nodded, miserably.

'We traced the call. We must take these things seriously. Can you please tell us what this was all about?'

'Nothing.' She fiddled with the sleeves of her jumper.

'It was a simple row,' I said, muttering that I'd get Matthew down to talk to them. I took the stairs two at a time, calling his name, but he didn't answer. The landing window was wide open. Oh my God, I thought, the idiot has jumped out. I ran downstairs again, and out into the garden, and found him white faced and shaking. 'I didn't do anything,' he said.

'I know. So, you've nothing to worry about.'

'But Bronagh…'

'Bronagh's explained. She said she over-reacted, so you're not in any trouble. At least you're not, if you come with me now, and talk to them.'

He hung back, but let me lead him in.

The policeman turned, and said, 'This young lady needs to come with us.'

'But I want to stay with Matthew,' she said, half smiling at him. 'I told you. He's done nothing wrong. We want to watch a movie.'

'You heard her,' I said. 'Let her stay. I can run her home later.'

'Sorry.' The policeman was firm. 'She made a complaint. She's coming with us.'

'But I don't want to.' Bronagh was close to tears.

'You have a choice.'

She looked up.

'You can come with us; we'll take you home safely, or, we can charge you for wasting police time.'

Bronagh paled. Picked up her coat, and, with a backward glance, she followed the police to their car.

When they'd gone, Matthew meandered out to the kitchen and I followed, to find him staring at the contents of the fridge. 'Are you all right?'

He nodded, so I said I had to go upstairs and work. I was distracted, because not only had I the new job with the local education authority, I had also to cover a shift for one of the youth workers, and I had some planning to do.

Before climbing the stairs, I gave Matthew a hug and told him I loved him and I would see him in the morning, just as I did every night.

'Can I get a new phone tomorrow?'

'We'll see,' I said, and he smiled, knowing that when I said, 'we'll see,' what I meant was 'yes.'

As I worked until the small hours, I was aware of Matthew pottering around downstairs, but I hadn't called out to him. I cursed myself for that now. Because that was the very last time that I saw him alive.

PART TWO: AFTER

6

The First Day

How do you cope when your firstborn dies? How can life continue? My mind shut down on that first morning, unable to process what had happened. My body took over, as if on automatic pilot.

After I had found Matthew; after I had called 999, my legs took me outside. I slumped down beside the garage, my mind blank, as I waited for the police to arrive. After a while I saw a police car speeding past the house. A minute or two passed before it came back again. I watched, as the doors flew open, then slammed shut, and two policewomen came running towards me. The older one, taking charge, shouted, 'Where is he? Where is your son?'

'He's out the back,' I said, pointing. 'He's in his room.' I had built the garage conversion especially for Matthew, as a bedroom separate from the rest of the house, sitting back into the garden. Wanting to keep him safe, under my roof, it was a way to give him the independence he so craved without the necessity for him to move out. It had proved a good compromise – or so I had thought.

Standing up, my legs feeling unsteady, I led the policewomen into his room. I hugged myself hard and tried not to look towards his bed. It was the first time, since I had found him, that I had ventured into his room. As the women checked Matthew over, I noticed the disturbing string, or cable tie, wrapped around his neck.

I was distracted by a fluttering noise and noticed a bird in the corner of the room.

'Look!' I said to the officers, pointing upwards.

The words had no sooner left my mouth, then the bird flew out, into the garden. I thought, how bizarre! I have witnessed birds flying into windows, banging off the glass, yet this one was able to fly through the narrow opening between Matthew's bedroom and the patio door. It had absolute precision. I watched, mesmerised. The bird, I strongly believe, was taking Matthew's soul to heaven. I had read that this is an Indian belief, and the thought gave me a little comfort. Later, remembering this, I researched all kinds of things on Google, looking for meanings in everyday occurrences.

I didn't want to look at my dead son; I couldn't bear to, but however much I resisted, my eyes were drawn to him. And it seemed that those eyes stared right back at me. I lost it then. I fell at his feet, sobbing; begging the policewomen to help him. And, noticing how traumatised I was, the older woman said to the younger, 'Take her back to the house. Stay with her. Stay with the mother.' She said this in such a matter of fact way. As if I was in the way – hampering her work. As if I was no one.

Tearing my eyes away from Matthew's, I stared at the older woman. I thought, sod you, you don't even care. You can't show real empathy. Then I followed the younger woman. I glanced back for a last look at Matthew as I left the room. 'I can't help you now,' I said, and the younger woman gave my arm a squeeze.

She led me back into the house, and followed me, then dropped back, staying a step behind me, like an obedient lapdog. She didn't let me out of her sight, following me from room to room, giving me no privacy. I complained, and she said,

'You're not to be on your own.'

I'm not sure what my girls were doing, but assumed that they were in Natasha's room, dressed and ready for whatever the day was about to throw at them. I wandered upstairs and saw them sitting on the bed looking white faced. They were good girls, I'd told them not to go outside, and they'd listened… or had they? I really hoped they had.

I thought of Matthew, downstairs. Dead with staring eyes, a dark blue mouth and protruding tongue. It was like a scene from a horror movie and was not something the girls should ever see.

I rang first. Our beautiful baby, Daniel was teething. This made him fretful, and Terry had taken him the night before so that I could get a decent night's sleep. He didn't pick up. When I rang my sister, she answered cheerily. But when I said, 'Matthew is dead,' she fell silent. After a few seconds, I wondered if she had hung-up. 'Hello?' I said. 'Are you still there?'

'Oh Sharon,' she said. 'I'm in the car. I'm taking the boys to school – you're on speakerphone.' She paused. 'I don't know what to say.'

But, how could she? There were no words.

Trying to retain a little normality, I went for a shower. 'Don't lock the door,' said the policewoman, hovering behind me, and I thought, oh, you care now, do you?' I don't know how long I stayed there, in the shower. It felt good, letting the hot water stream over my hair and my body. I turned it up, wanting the water to scald me. As if physical pain would take away the deeper agony. And as long as I was there, I didn't have to face the truth. The questions. The sympathy.

My sister's brother-in-law was the first to arrive. He came in and, putting his arms around me, said how sorry he was. I'm not an emotional person and I was thinking, why are you hugging me? I'd been taught, as a child, that showing emotion was a sign of weakness. I've learned to wait until I'm alone to cry, with just God as a witness.

I tried ringing Terry again. I left a message and cursed him for not being there when I needed him. Then Natasha tried him; she dialled again and again, but it went to voicemail each time. After that I phoned James. Before I could say a word, he said, 'What's Matthew done now?' He sounded distracted, and said he was on the way to work.

'Your son is dead,' I said, and there was silence on the line. Then, almost whispering, he muttered, 'I'm on my way.'

He arrived with his brother-in-law Gary. They came into the kitchen, and before I could say a word, muttered that killing yourself was an idiot thing to do. I saw red.

'I don't know why I even bothered to ring you,' I said. 'You did fuck all for him in life.'

'That's not fair, Sharon,' said Gary, giving me a sharp look.

'Come on Gary,' I said. 'You didn't even let the boys hang around together.' His son, Stuart, and Matthew were best buddies, but Gary thought Matthew was a bad influence. Had he only known it; Matthew had dug his cousin out of trouble on more than one occasion.

James's expression darkened, and I saw him clench his fists. For a minute I thought he was going to hit me, but Gary pulled him away and the moment passed. The two of them went outside and sat in Gary's van, talking, but making no move to drive away.

The phone rang. It was Darren, Matthew's boss from the furniture shop, asking why Matthew was late.

'He's not answering his phone,' he said. 'Would it help if I came and picked him up.'

'I don't think he's coming to work today.' I said it calmly.

'Why not?'

'Matthew is dead.'

I put the phone down, not wanting to have to say how he died. And before I knew it, Darren's van drew up. I went outside to meet him, and he ran towards me, threw his arms around me, and sobbed on my shoulder. Why was this grown man crying? I looked at him dispassionately, thinking, why are *you* so distraught, when it's *my* son.

He walked into the house joining my brother in law, and my sister, who, having dropped her children at school, had rushed over. I continued to inform friends and family, working through my mobile from A-Z. Then I walked in, meeting Darren on his way out. But almost immediately, there was a knock on the door. I was delighted to see Wilma, my wonderful and supportive next-door neighbour, back from her walk with the dogs. Taking my hands between hers, she said, 'Sharon, what's happened? I saw the police car.'

I said, 'Matthew's dead,' and she cried. And I wondered why I couldn't join her. Why was it that I was dry eyed? Was I normal?

'What can I do?'

'You could go up and talk to the girls,' I said, and nodding she took to the stairs. Wilma is the best! One of the nicest, sincere and genuine people I have ever met. She never had children of her own, but she's like an auntie to mine. She was mad about horses – just like fifteen-year-old Natasha, and the two of them would talk forever.

In the next few hours the house began to fill. Mark, Annie-Jean's Dad arrived. We have a good and easy relationship now, and I'm not sure, why we broke up. Perhaps it was because, after the hurt and pain of previous relationships we couldn't move on. I think we were afraid to fully trust each other and didn't believe that things could be different. Thankfully, we've remained good friends. He's a great dad to Annie Jean, and his elder children, Rebekah and Nathan are devoted to their younger sister.

'Is there anything I can do?' he asked.

'I don't know,' I said. 'I can't think.'

'Can I contact anyone for you?'

'My mother,' I said. She had rung me earlier, responding to a message from Natasha. She knew something had happened to her adored grandson, but I hadn't been able to tell her he was dead. Not over the phone.

She kept phoning, sounding more and more distraught, and I said I'd be down to her shortly. But she didn't take that as an answer. She kept saying, 'Tell me now.'

So, I did. Through my tears I said, 'Matthew is dead. He killed himself.'

'No Sharon,' she said. 'He wouldn't do that. Not Matthew. Let me talk to him.'

Did she think I was joking? *Would* anyone joke about something like that?

'Could you go down there?' I asked Mark. 'Take Annie Jean with you, and just be with her?'

He agreed, and they drove off. The phone rang again immediately. It was Mum.

'I'm driving up,' she said, and I told her not to; but to wait for Mark and Annie Jean.

'The police are with Matthew,' I said. 'They're going to take him away.'

'Take him away?' she sounded indignant. 'Where to?'

'I don't know. Some coroner's office I think.'

'Why?'

'To see why he died.'

'When?'

'Soon, I think.'

I couldn't bear her questions. All I wanted was the house to myself, and to wake up from this nightmare. Because deep down, I didn't really believe that Matthew was dead. How could he be? The police hadn't said the words, and I was waiting with a spark of hope.

My next concerns were how the girls, Bronagh and Shanice would take the news. There was no reply from Bronagh's phone, and when I couldn't get hold of Shanice, I rang her mum and gave her an earful. After blaming her for not keeping her daughter away from my son, I told her that I didn't want Shanice at the funeral. By the time Shanice phoned back, I'd calmed down and I apologised to her. It was not for me to make that decision.

The news spread, and the house filled. My friends rallied round. I'd rung them, one after the other, sitting in the garden to get a signal. It was so hard. I dialled, and, in an effort to hold back tears, kept my voice even, and emotionless. 'Matthew is dead. He took his own life.' I'd say the words, and in the silence that followed, say that I had other calls to make.

My friends were wonderful; especially Karen, Roberta and Tina, friends who mean a lot to me. We take off now and then, for a weekend in Berlin or somewhere, and without being asked, they fell into line.

My closest friend from university, Kritti came from Newcastle upon Tyne. Karen collected her from the airport, and they arrived in, with supermarket bags overflowing. They threw themselves into the organisation, as if they dealt with death every day. Their support was so valuable – I really do not think I could have coped without them.

Thanks to Karen, there was drink for everyone; and lots of fizzy drink for Matthew's friends. Karen's sister, Rosemary wanted a job, and she was sent to get a bottle of Baileys for me. When she handed me a glass, saying, 'drink this,' I couldn't help laughing. I'm not a drinker.

'You do know this is a depressant,' I said, but I drank it, anyway.

Wilma eventually went home – and returned with trays and trays overflowing with cheese and pickle sandwiches. Greenfields Nursery, where Daniel attended when I started work when Daniel was 10 weeks old, sent homemade buns and cupcakes, supplied extra chairs, and urged us to make full use of their carpark. A procession of people I didn't recognise walked up to the house and left cards of sympathy.

I sat in the room, unable to function, whilst Karen made everyone welcome. I spoke to those who approached me, and from time to time went to Matthew, to give him a kiss. My house; my place of safety felt alien. Being there felt unsafe, and I was afraid.

I couldn't see Kritti; but when I wandered out to the kitchen to fetch myself a glass of water, I found her on her knees, surrounded by saucepans, cleaning out a cupboard. Seeing me, she smiled, and said, 'It's not that your house isn't clean – but, this makes me feel useful.' I had to laugh.

Natasha stayed out of the way, holed in her room with her friends. When she was younger, she and Matthew, being close in age had clashed. But recently, I'd noticed they had become closer. At least, generally they had. But sometimes, Matthew overdid the caring.

Just weeks before, she'd come home from school, fuming! 'They won't leave me alone,' she'd said.

'Who won't?'

'Matthew. And Stuart,' she added, naming their cousin. Throwing herself down on the couch, she said, 'I was talking to this guy from school; just talking, and the two of them kept driving by to spy on me.' She snorted.

'They mean well,' I said. 'They're just trying to protect you.'

She raised her eyebrows. 'Well they shouldn't bother. I can look after myself.'

It wasn't the first time Matthew had looked out for her. Natasha has inherited her grandmother's genes – and looks more Chinese than the rest of us. When she first moved to secondary school, she was bullied for this.

Furious, Matthew stepped in and put an end to it. He knew, only too well, what such verbal abuse felt like. After all, he, too, had been bullied, until, with the support of others, he had learned to stick up for himself, and gained the reputation as someone not to be messed with. There was no way he was going to let his sister suffer as he had.

Annie Jean – my precious girl of just eight years old, who loved her brother so very much, became the practical one. She adored Matthew. They shared a love of music and danced together to their favourite tracks. Just the week before I'd heard the laughter as the two of them sang along to, 'I'm Sexy and I know it.'

How did she find the strength to become 'the mother?' Acquiring, from somewhere, a hardback notebook, she asked everyone who crossed the threshold to sign their names, and she became the perfect hostess; going around serving everyone with tea, coffee, sandwiches and biscuits.

And me? I sat in a corner, stunned with shock, not crying; yet feeling inwardly dead; as if my heart had died along with the son that I loved. Time was suspended. I was just there. The worst thing was knowing that Matthew was still in his room; still staring vacantly into space. Part of me was haunted by him; the other part wanted to be back there with him, holding him one last time.

In the afternoon, I saw a black car pull up. The policewomen came to tell me they were taking Matthew away. These men in black suits got out of the car, and walked, unsmiling, towards Matthew's room. The sight of them – like something out of a macabre movie – made me shiver. I couldn't bear the thought of seeing them take him – it was just too much, so I pulled the blinds down. But as I was doing so, I caught a glimpse of the black body bag, being hauled out to the waiting car. And, at that exact moment, Mark arrived, my mother in the passenger seat. I cried out in alarm.

She saw the body of the grandson she had adored, and I rushed out to protect her, but she was focused on the men; and, approaching them, asked where they were taking Matthew to. They told her, and she asked what time he'd be back – as calmly as if he was just popping out for a coffee. Getting her answer, she made her way to Matthew's room and sat there, waiting for his return. We could hear her from the living room, crying, howling like an injured animal.

Karen, rising from the couch, went out to comfort her. After a minute or so, she brought my mother through to us, speaking to her quietly. I knew how much she was hurting and didn't know how I could take away her pain. But my friends, taking care to talk to her, proved a great distraction. Even so, she kept disappearing into Matthew's room.

After dinner, the house filled up with well-wishers. My mother sat in the new second sitting room, which I'd converted from the dining room, intending it for Matthew's visiting friends.

Part of me still didn't believe that Matthew was dead. Even though I'd seen him – and knew the body in that bag was his. Bizarrely, nobody had actually told me he was dead. All day I had been waiting for the police to announce it to me, formally, and they never said it. In my heart, he was still alive.

Turning back into the sitting room, I noticed how crowded it had become. In one way that was gratifying. It showed how many people cared, except, that some of those who were sitting around, eating sandwiches didn't care. Or so I thought.

I saw my ex father in law, Jim, sitting in the living room as I was walking out of the kitchen. What the hell was *he* doing here? He didn't love his grandson – he didn't even know him. When I'd first met James, Jim had already bailed out of the marriage, and he hadn't shown a shred of interest in either Matthew or Natasha.

Just three months before Matthew died, Matthew and Natasha had been walking the dogs across a field opposite our house when a van stopped and asked the way to the local vet. They told me, later, that it was Jim, but he hadn't even recognised them – his own grandchildren. It had been so long since he'd set eyes on them - so what was he doing in my house, now that his grandson was dead, and it was all too late?

There were others there who clearly *did* care. And amongst them, at last, was Terry. Hugging him, I said, 'I didn't hear you sneak in.' Just having him there calmed me a little. Pointing out Jim, pouring out my feelings, I asked Terry to talk to him for me. 'I don't know why he's here,' I explained, 'so I don't know what to say.'

'Some people will come,' he said. 'It's just the way it is. But it says more about him than about you.'

Shanice was the last one to leave. It was well after midnight, and I took myself off to bed. Did I sleep at all? If I did, it wasn't for long. Because every time I closed my eyes, I saw Matthew's eyes staring at me in death. The alarm jarred, going off at 6.30am. I stayed in bed, staring at the ceiling, trying to make my mind go blank. I concentrated on the spider's web, but it was no good. I was frozen with fear. And I didn't get up until 7.21. Exactly the same time as the day before. How would I get through another day?

7

Saying Goodbye

Matthew's friends were nervous about the wake. Traumatised by his death, they weren't sure what to do. They'd hesitated before coming to the house; and a carload of them had arrived first thing on Friday morning, asking me could they attend the house, or was the wake just for adults?

'Of course, you can come. You're welcome,' I said. 'You're his friends. But wait until this afternoon when Matthew will be here.'

They looked at me, puzzled for a second or two, then realisation dawned. 'You mean?'

'His body will be here.'

'I'm sorry we didn't come yesterday.' This was Jamie. 'But when I saw the message on Facebook, I just didn't believe it. I thought it was a sick joke and warned the person to remove it.' Then he admitted he'd used extremely strong language.

I half smiled. 'I don't think Natasha would much appreciate that.'

'Natasha? It wasn't her post.' He mentioned another friend, and I realised the news had been widely shared.

Another of Matthew's friends, Nick, arrived by taxi with his girlfriend. He was concerned about what to wear for the funeral. 'Do I need to get a suit?' he asked.

'Just wear whatever feels comfortable,' I said.

I was dreading my afternoon meeting with Wray Funeral Directors, and it wasn't easy. My sister suggested I should get James involved. 'I know you're angry with him,' she said. 'I know he could have been a better father, but he's lost his son. You must let him help.'

I saw the sense in that, and when he and Tina, arrived, I asked him if he'd like to pick some clothes to take to the funeral parlour. He came out with a red shirt and good jeans. 'Is this ok?' he asked, and I nodded.

'Would you like to come to come to the parlour with us?' I asked them, and they said they would. The four of us drove down in two different cars. And we sat there, in that strangely silent place, and it didn't feel real. I was there, but in my head I wasn't. Not really. The funeral director was good to us and patient, and that made it easier. He talked about Matthew in the present tense and was extremely respectful. But it was tough when he asked us what we wanted, because we had different ideas. Handing us catalogues, he asked us which coffin we'd like and which flowers.

'Well it depends,' said James. '

'Depends on what?' I gave him a sharp look.

'On the cost,' he said.

That shocked me, and ignoring him, I picked out a pine coffin with gold handles and a raised lid. 'And I'd like a mixture of yellow roses and carnations to lie over the coffin,' I added.

'I'd like to have the funeral in our garden,' I said. 'It's an old allotment garden on three levels – it's really long. I think that's what Matthew would have liked.'

They agreed that it would be all right. Then we discussed the plot in the graveyard, and that's when the fun began.

'I gather you purchased two plots last year?'

I agreed that I had. My mother had been unwell, and it had seemed like a good idea. Back then, they had shown me the map of the graveyard, and I'd chosen plots close to the toilets. I'd thought that would be handy for anyone visiting the graves. It had made perfect sense to me.

'We've had a call from the council office, wondering if you'd like to change the position of the plots.'

'Why would I want to do that?' I was mystified.

He looked uncomfortable and ran his finger between his neck and the collar of his shirt. 'The ones you chose are on the wrong side of the graveyard.'

I looked at him in consternation. 'I'm sorry? The wrong side?'

'The Catholic side.'

I hadn't known this but didn't care. I explained that I'd simply chosen the sites that were nearest to the toilets, and told him why, but this clarification only added to his confusion.

'It's the first I've heard of it,' said James, giving me a hard, disapproving stare. 'And Matthew's *not* Catholic.'

'I'm well aware of that,' I said. 'And I'm aware that some of my family over here are Presbyterian. But I'm half Chinese with family in Singapore. Some of them are Catholic; some Buddhist. So, unless there is a specific plot for someone like me, I'm going to keep the plot I've bought, thank you very much.'

This really mattered to me, if only because Matthew had seen it. I'd driven the children up there to show them the plot. He would expect to be buried there.

I was determined to stay strong, but I didn't feel it. I'd never had to 'do' death before and was confused enough about the practicalities without this extra complication. If my beliefs didn't fit anywhere in the graveyard, did I then, no longer fit in the world?

James and Tina didn't say another word, but I could see that James still wasn't happy. And I wasn't altogether surprised when I had a call from his mother, Joyce, later that afternoon.

'I've heard what you've done,' she said. 'And I'm horrified.'

'About the graves, you mean?' I explained my reasoning, once again.

'If that's your final word, Sharon, I have to tell you that nobody from this side of the family will be attending the funeral.'

'That's ok then,' I said. 'It's your choice.'

I kept my voice firm, determined that she wouldn't catch any moment of weakness, but inside I was falling to pieces. Would it be simpler to simply give in? Why did it matter? Why did *any* of this matter. The only issue was that Matthew was dead, and that he was not coming back. Not ever.

When Wray's rang later, I steeled myself for more questions about the plot, but they had rung about another matter. 'We've been thinking about your choice of venue,' the funeral director said.

'The garden? You said that would be ok?'

'We don't object to it, but there's likely to be quite a crowd attending the funeral, so perhaps you should reconsider?'

There was no fight left in me, so I asked what he would suggest. And agreed, without further argument, that it should take place in the church at Wray's Funeral Parlour in Antrim.

'We can have speakers,' he said. 'Then if there are too many people to fit in the church, they will still be able to hear what is going on.' He paused, then said. 'We'll have Matthew back with you this afternoon, as arranged, if that's still convenient?'

My heart missed a beat. I was nervous of seeing Matthew again. I wondered what he would look like. Would his eyes still stare? Would his tongue still protrude, and his lips still be blue? When the open coffin arrived, and was placed in Matthew's room, I approached it with a great deal of trepidation. I looked down at him and breathed out, almost faint with relief. In his red shirt and blue jeans, he looked like the live Matthew I loved so much. I thanked Wray's, remarking on what an incredible job they had done.

I noticed that Matthews's mirror was turned to the wall and asked why.

'It's unlucky to have a mirror in the room with the coffin,' the funeral director said.

This puzzled me, and later, intrigued, I googled this, and read that some people believe the person's soul can be trapped in the mirror. The thought haunted me, and I left the mirror facing the wall long after Matthew's body had vacated his room. I was afraid to look into it in case I saw Matthew staring back at me.

It's hard for anyone to view a dead body, so I gave Natasha and Annie-Jean the choice. I asked them did they want to see Matthew; did they want to place anything in his coffin? 'I've put in a photo of us all,' I said. 'Would you like to add anything?'

Anne-Jean smiled. 'I've written a poem about Matthew,' she said. 'I'd like to put that in. When she placed it in the coffin, and looked at her brother, a sense of calm came over her. She said she was glad she'd seen him.

Natasha was uneasy about seeing her brother. I wondered why, until Annie-Jean took me to one side. 'Mum, we saw him.'

'What?'

'Yesterday. We saw him.' She shuddered.

I was horrified. 'But I told you not to go outside,' I said. I warned you.'

She hung her head, and said, 'We had to take Buster out.'

'But you didn't.' I was confused. 'There was no need. I'd already taken him out.'

I encouraged Natasha to see her brother now that the undertakers had worked on him. It might take away the horrific image of the newly dead Matthew. She was still reluctant, and whilst Annie-Jean came in and out of the room with me, with ease, watching as I talked to my son and kissed him, it took Natasha a while to pluck up courage. She waited until her friends were there to support her and went in with them.

The children had never attended a funeral before, so I explained what happens, and made sure that they were happy to be present – and both were.

The doctor had prescribed some diazepam for me – I'd never taken it before – well, I had never needed to. It had a very strange effect on me. That evening, I sat in a corner, by myself, not sure whether to laugh or cry. The room went bleary, as if I was looking at it through a fog.

In that state, I wasn't, at first, aware of all that was going on in our full house. I knew that Shanice and Bronagh had both visited – they had begged to be allowed to, and I hadn't the heart to stop them. But everyone else, it seemed, was against them. Matthew's friends felt they had been the main cause of his problems and were not being especially friendly to them. And as rivals, they kept clear of each other.

Once I got wind of this, I decided to intervene. Walking in to the second living room, I was distracted by the sight of four young men – Matthew's closest friends, Gregory, Kenny, Ricky and Richard, sitting in a row wearing suits. Momentarily forgetting my troubles, I felt a bubble of laughter escape. 'You guys look as if you're auditioning for X-Factor,' I said.

'We wanted to show respect,' muttered Gregory with an embarrassed smile.

'No, it's great,' I said. 'But there's something I have to say to you.'

'Oh?'

'It's about Shanice and Bronagh.'

They looked at each other with warily.

'I understand how you feel about the girls,' I said. 'But right or wrong, Matthew loved both of them, and out of respect for Matthew – and for me – you have to make those girls feel welcome. Do you understand?'

They nodded. I went around to all the other friend groups, saying the same to them. And to give them credit, they did make an effort.

If the teenagers proved easy to handle, my mum proved harder. When she set eyes on Bronagh, it was all I could do to stop her approaching to give her a piece of her mind. 'And I suppose that Shanice is here too,' she said, in a voice that carried, alarmingly. When I nodded, and tried to explain why, she cut across me, and said, 'I just don't want them here. It's not right.'

Calling Karen and My aunt Vilma over, I explained the situation and said, 'Could you try and distract my mum – keep her away from the girls?'

Vilma proved a wonderful support, yet I'd only met her the previous year. I'd been searching for my cousins, Samuel and Neil on Facebook, and she responded. She lived an hour's drive away but would come over whenever I needed her. We'd become close.

They glanced at each other, nervously, and I said, 'Mission impossible, I know! But could you do your best?'

They were great at distracting Mum. They took her to the kitchen – or the main living room on the pretence that someone wanted to speak to her, in order to keep the peace, and avoid any ugly scenes. In truth, I think Mum blamed *me* for Matthew's death. But she didn't say as much. Not right then.

Having read Matthew's friends the riot act, I asked them would they like a drink to toast their late friend with? Because grateful though I was for their restrained behaviour, it seemed unnatural to see them drinking tea.

I felt I could trust them not to disgrace themselves, and my confidence was not misplaced. They drank just one can each, disappearing into the garden to toast Matthew, and when, later, after everyone had gone, I went into the garden to clear up, I was astounded, not to say happy, that they had left it pristine. All the beer cans – and all the cigarette stubs had been tidily thrown away.

I mentioned it to Natasha, saying how heartened I was that Matthew's friends respected me so much, and she laughed.

'What's so funny?' I asked.

'It's not *you* they respect,' she said. 'I mean, they do respect you, but they were tidying up for Matthew.'

'How come?'

'You know what a clean freak Matthew was,' she said. 'He was always giving people grief. When we came back with fish and chips, he'd send everyone outside, because he could not bear the mess in his room.'

That night, I was sleepless, yet again. And as I lay there, I went through, in my mind, all that had happened; and I wondered, yet again, what I could have done to make things different.

The following morning, the house was, blessedly, free of visitors. Mum was there – sitting with Matthew, crying, when the doorbell rang. I answered. It was Maeve, my manager from work, and Pamela, a colleague. 'We've come to pay our respects,' they said, speaking quietly, saying how sorry they were. I offered them coffee, and they followed me out of the room. Mum shouted after us.

'It's all *your* fault Sharon,' she said. 'If you hadn't let that Bronagh visit, my grandson would still be alive.'

I stood still, shocked. But she hadn't finished her tirade. 'You knew Matthew was upset that night, and you didn't check on him.'

I sighed, and just took it. I understood her anger; the events of Matthew's last night had clearly been playing on her mind. It made her antipathy towards Shanice and Bronagh so easy to understand. My colleague, though, was shocked. She put her arm round me. 'Sharon don't listen to her. That's terrible. How can she say that? Everyone knows you did everything you could.'

I *did f*eel shaken. And her words had made me feel even more guilty than I did already.

'You do know it's not your fault,' she added.

'It's ok,' I said, switching on the kettle and setting out mugs. 'She's hurting so much. If it helps her to blame me, that's ok. I can take it.'

I lay in bed on the morning of the funeral, Monday 15 October, thinking about Matthew, and about the day ahead. How could I bear it? It was one thing getting through Thursday and Friday. I'd somehow stumbled through the weekend. But today? The day I had to bury my son? How in the world would I be able to cope with that?

I took 2 diazepam to dull the ache of grief. It's not something I had ever done before, but if the pills could help me stay strong – or at least help me hide my feelings from others – any sign of weakness, that, I reasoned, was okay.

Preparing to dress in black added to the sombreness of my mood. But that moment turned to panic, when I tried pulling up the zip of my black dress, and it wouldn't close. 'What will I do?' I said, wishing I had gone shopping with James's half-sister Leigh – who had taken Natasha to get *her* kitted out.

'Stand still,' said Kritti. 'It's just a caught thread.' She pulled it out, and all was well. Annie-Jean came in looking pretty, in a black pinafore dress.

'Is Natasha back yet?' I asked.

'Yup. Auntie Leigh drove in a few minutes ago. Natasha's got black trousers and a jacket.'

'So, she's happy?' Annie Jean nodded as I reached for my black coat. 'That's good.'

When we arrived at Wray's at 10.25am, just in time for the service, we were amazed to see a crowd of people standing outside. Seeing us, they stood back to allow us to walk in, to take our places at the front.

We had wonderful speakers in Darren Pearson and Rodney Agnew from the Green Pastures Church. And we'd picked lovely wee songs. We had 'The Lord's My Shepherd,' and 'Amazing Grace.' But the organist kept missing the notes. I found that bizarre. I raised my eyebrows at Terry.

'The organist rang in sick,' he whispered.

'What?' I assumed he was serious. 'So, who is this?'

He shrugged. 'They picked him up from the shopping centre,' he said.

I laughed – or started to and turned it into a cough. But the more I held in my laughter, the more it escaped. I knew it would look odd, but I couldn't stop. Influenced by diazepam, I wasn't sure if I was laughing at each missed note, or the fact that, for a minute, I'd thought that Terry was telling me the truth.

Annie Jean read her poem – a copy of the one she had placed in the coffin with Matthew. It was beautiful. She wrote it herself - a rhyming poem about Matthew's different hair styles; about his favourite songs, and about the dance moves he taught her, or as she would say, she taught him.

Some of Matthew's friends had asked if they could carry the coffin, so it was arranged. And at the service's end, as they carried Matthew down the aisle, we played, *We Are Young,* by Fun.

It fitted so perfectly! I nodded my thanks to my sister, Maria, who had suggested the song was appropriate. Matthew had loved it. It became my kind of grief anthem. Hearing it always brings me close to Matthew.

Following Matthew out of the church, I noticed that the crowd had grown considerably, and the bulk of those gathering to pay their respects were young. All these teenagers, girls and boys, had cared for Matthew, and they were all distraught. It was a reminder, as if I needed one, that Matthew was so much more than his problems. The life and soul of any party, he was loved. As we left for the graveyard, Mark struck up on the pipes, and the mournful sound made the moment more poignant still.

I had thought that Matthew's friends would soon tire – and had imagined that the coffin would be transferred into the hearse for the journey to the graveyard. But we ended up walking the whole mile, because so many of the 100 or so people walking behind me, wanted a turn carrying their friend home. I was overwhelmed by their support.

I was hoping that the pastor would take this opportunity to open the door of the church to all these young people, by saying something meaningful, and comforting, but his message was all about the need to be saved. This didn't feel appropriate.

I go to church. I'm a believer, and I wondered if my son *was* going to heaven. He wasn't, as far as I could see, 'Saved,' in the way the pastor was explaining, but he had been christened. He knew the stories from the bible and he believed them. I hoped that was enough. We kept saying, 'Alleluia', as a response to the pastor's words, hoping, desperately, that he would soon stop talking, but he didn't, not for ages.

As I was pondering this, it was time to lower Matthew into the ground. Watching him below me, in the earth, I had a mad impulse to jump in right after him. It took all my willpower to stay, standing with the others. Taking a deep breath to steady myself, I threw a white rose onto the coffin to signify the innocence of my young boy, who took his own life because he didn't know what else to do.

The young girls who attended, had other ideas. They each carried a single rainbow coloured rose – signifying the fun and colour Matthew created around himself. The sight of them all made me made me realise that my precious boy had united the community. It was a wonderful gesture, and the rose, has become thought of as 'Matthew's Rose.'

I'd had enough, and wished that everyone would magically disappear, so that I could say goodbye to my son in peace. But I had to keep on my public face and shake hands with all the mourners who queued up to say, 'I'm sorry for your loss.'

James's family *had* come to the funeral, in spite of their misgivings. Wondering what James was feeling, burying his son, I remembered how, once, I had really loved him. And I felt sad that a relationship that had started so well could go so very badly wrong.

8

Shock

After the funeral, when I closed my door, I was left on my own. Nobody visited. And although there were times, I needed to be alone, as the days and first week or two went by, I missed the support of neighbours, friends and family, and especially of the young people. It was hard. One minute the house was bursting at the seams, the next there was a hollow emptiness.

Those were the darkest of dark days. When Natasha and Annie Jean had left for school, I'd go into Matthew's room, and sit on his bed, in the place where he had died, where I had found him. That moment never left me. It didn't matter what time I woke up, I would lie in bed, each day, until 7.21am – the time I had found Matthew. I was scared to get up sooner. That continued for years – which was mad, when the clocks had meanwhile changed several times over.

It was torment, imagining his last moments. I'd hold my breath, counting the seconds; trying to work out how long it took him to die. I'd wonder what his last thought had been. Was he thinking of Shanice? Of the baby Bronagh was expecting? Did he stop to wonder, just for a second, how I would feel when I found him? Or was he in such pain that he didn't think at all?

I'd sit there in a state of numbness, sometimes remaining all day, not moving, until it was time to collect the girls from school and Daniel from day-care. Then I'd dry my tears, find the car keys, and drag myself away.

There were lighter moments. My brother works at sea, but he had flown back for the funeral, returning to his ship soon afterwards. He'd taken a part in the proceedings, and had carried the coffin, but was paired up with someone considerably shorter than he was. When he came home to visit, during those first dark days, he was wearing a wrist support.

'What have you done to yourself?'

He laughed. 'I hurt it at Matthew's funeral.'

'What? How?'

'I had to take all the weight to keep the coffin at the right angle,' he said. 'I didn't realise that the handles were purely ornamental, and didn't the handle break off?'

'What?' I laughed.

'So, there I was, trying to balance the coffin with one hand, and screw on the handle with the other.'

Later, returning from his first visit to see Matthew at the cemetery, he said he'd taken flowers. 'I thought, I'd have a joke with him, and I took him pink roses,' he said. 'But when I opened that sachet, they give you to feed the flowers with, it splashed all over my best Hugo Boss shirt.' He roared with laughter. 'So, I reckon your Matthew had the last laugh. Typical!'

Great though such moments of humour were, they were few and far between. I hated leaving Matthew's room, and found it almost impossible to visit the local shops, to see ordinary life going on. It seemed strange that whilst, for me, life was over, for others it went on as normal. That hurt. It made me want to scream.

I'd wait until the fridge was empty, and only then force myself to Tesco. The outside world seemed so strange. Colours were brighter; noises were heightened, and, feeling numb, I imagined I was living in an alternative reality.

I'd have thought I was invisible, except that people's reaction to me was so pronounced. They'd see me, all right, but immediately turn their heads, and scuttle down a different aisle to avoid having to talk to me.

One time, returning from Ballymena, I told Terry how I felt. 'Why is everyone talking and laughing as if life was normal?' I said. 'How can they do that when my son has just died?'

Terry pulled me into a hug. 'Sharon,' he said, stroking my long hair, 'That was you in the week before Matthew died. When you were getting on with your normal life, somebody else's child, or husband or wife had died. And they felt the same about your attitude.'

I understood that, but it didn't help. I still didn't go out at all, except when it was absolutely necessary. I was too afraid that insensitive people would say the wrong thing, or that there would be a trigger; something to remind me of Matthew.

There was that first time I heard an ambulance, and the siren frightened me to death; the first time I saw a hearse – the men in black bringing back that first, most terrible of days. There was that afternoon when I took Daniel to a play area and saw cable-ties securing padding on the trampoline. That one, bringing back the image of Matthew, grotesque in death, gave me such acute palpitations, that I slumped down on a bench, momentarily fighting for breath.

One time, I was with Terry in Ballymena buying some petrol. When he went into the garage to pay, I noticed some lads sitting on the railings, their backs to me. One of them was the image of Matthew. He had the same haircut – shaved at the back and over his ears.

My heart stopped. It was my son standing there. He was not dead after all, and he was carefree, just enjoying being with his friends. For a moment I was happy, lost in the illusion that this really was Matthew. I prayed that the lad would not look round, because when he did, I would have to acknowledge that he wasn't Matthew. I'd have to go back to that place of pain.

I wasn't the only one suffering; we all were. Annie Jean has always been open natured, and happy to share her feelings. I'd been dropping her at school one day and noticed that she was upset. 'What's wrong?' I asked.

'I didn't get to say goodbye to Matthew,' she said, blowing her nose.

'Yes, you did,' I said. 'Surely you did. You were in and out of that room with me.'

'Yeah, but on the day of the funeral, when I went in to say my real goodbye, it was too late. The funeral directors were there.' She started to cry again.

Worried about her, realising I wasn't the best person to see her through this, I organised counselling for her. I asked the school for support to provide a school counsellor but they were unable to assist. That meant I had to take her outside school during school times, which caused stress all round. I was disappointed that they didn't offer her that much needed support. After all, Annie Jean was only 8 years old.

I offered Natasha counselling too, but she refused it. Yet, in my mind, she was the one who needed it most. One day, clambering into the car, throwing her schoolbag down, she noticed that I was wearing Matthew's socks, and told me it looked stupid. I explained that I wore them in order to feel closer to Matthew, but she wasn't listening. Shouting at me, her anger escalating, she said, 'You're a rubbish mother.'

That shook me, but I tried not to take it to heart, because everything made Natasha angry back then. She was young, and she was scared. And besides, it was true; I was too traumatised to be the greatest mother right then, but I *was* doing my best. I watched my children's emotional behaviour, often expressed through music or the games they played, and I tried to give them space to talk about Matthew. Did I really deserve her abuse?

She was silent for the rest of the journey home, but when we arrived, and entered the kitchen her anger exploded. 'You wish it had been *me*, don't you?' she said.

'What?'

'You wish *I* had died, instead of your precious Matthew!'

'That's just not true – you know it's not!' I reached out to her, wanting to give her a hug, and tell her how much I loved her, but she didn't give me a chance. Stomping off to her room, she slammed the door behind her. I sat down, covering my face in my hands with despair. When I took them away, there was a cup of tea on the table, made for me by Annie Jean. She was the strong one. Perhaps she had to be.

Natasha's mood failed to lift. She spent most of her time, up in her room, hidden away, thinking dark thoughts. And when I went into her room to collect her dirty washing, I stopped dead, horrified. She had written messages all over her white walls in black eyeliner. Messages of hate to me, and to Matthew, cursing him for dying. 'I wish you were here with me, Matthew, and not Mum,' she wrote. And worse still, 'I wish I was dead!' It was like a scene from a horror movie and was beyond my worst imaginings.

I looked for help from social services, and after a week, they called out. But when they learned that I'd spoken to Natasha's friends, asking them to lend their support – and spoken to the children's form teachers asking that the girls could have time out, if things got too tough, they said I had already done the things they would advise me to do.

'Have the girls received counselling', they asked.

'Annie Jean has, but Natasha's not keen,' I told them.

They left some leaflets detailing what grief is and listing on-line sites for counselling. They suggested that Natasha might feel more comfortable with that. 'Don't worry. You're doing the right thing,' they said. 'You've clearly got a good relationship with your daughters. Give Natasha time.'

Those words haunted me. I'd heard them before. Many times, before, when I was being reassured about Matthew. And look where that ended? And it wasn't *just* that. I'd read the research, and I knew that the risk for girls of completing suicide was higher, if their brother had already done so.

Shortly afterwards things *did* improve. Natasha began to go out again. She'd hang out with Matthew's friends, trying to hold onto the brother she'd lost. I was pleased at this sign that she was ready to face the world again. I was pleased, but I was anxious, too. Would she be safe? I'd watch the clock, worrying if she was just one minute late. I worried when she was at home, too.

One Saturday, though, when she was out, I got a call from my nephew Terrell warning me I was in for a shock. And when Natasha walked into the kitchen, some hours later, I was glad of the call. Half of her beautiful long dark hair had been shaved off, and without the warning, I would have reacted with horror. Instead, I was able to hide my distress, and say, 'You look like Rhianna!'

'Do you want to feel it?' she smiled, presenting me with the shaved half of her head. Then, noticing my puzzlement, she said, 'It feels like Matthew's hair.'

My heart broke for her.

I felt sad for Daniel too. He had loved Matthew. When his big brother came into a room, the toddler would hold out his chubby arms, ready to be picked up. He was too young to understand what had happened, but he knew that something was wrong. He started waking at night and was hard to settle.

Terry was my rock. He'd look after Daniel in the evenings, so that I could rest. Little did he know that I *couldn't* rest. That instead of sleeping, I'd be thinking about Matthew, and researching where he had gone. I searched suicide support groups and looked at his Facebook page messages. Every now and then, I'd leave the screen, and go and check on the girls – just to make sure that they were still breathing.

Looking after Daniel in the daytimes, I'd watch him, and feel sick with worry. He was learning to walk, tottering a few steps before falling – and instead of celebrating his prowess, I watched anxiously, terrified that he would harm himself. It was like walking on eggshells; but I knew, rationally, I had to encourage him to meet his milestones.

And meanwhile, I counted the days, pleased, each night, that I'd managed to get myself through another twenty-four hours. It was like Groundhog Day – every day the same.

I had progressed a little. I managed the chores, somehow; dragging myself out, hoping I wouldn't come face to face with anyone I knew. I was worried they would talk about Matthew – and resentful if they did not. I couldn't move on from that morning I had found him. I'd see him as I'd found him every time, I closed my eyes.

I managed the shopping, somehow, but I did it in a robotic state. I'd get to the checkout and discover all these bars of chocolate in my trolley, along with Matthew's favourite biscuits. I'd stare at them, wondering how they had got there, but I never returned them to the shelves. I'd take them home to join the biscuits I'd bought for him the week before, and the week before that. I went out of my way to visit the bakery which sold Matthew's favourite sausage rolls. It wasn't logical. Natasha thought I'd lost my reason, but it helped to keep him close to me.

My emotions veered dangerously. I was annoyed with Matthew for dying, yet guilty that I hadn't done more to stop him. I was angry with CAMHS for not intervening, and I was scared of the night times. Even praying had its worrying side. I'd always asked God to keep my children safe. In taking Matthew, had he thought that he was protecting him? Would he take my other children in order to keep them safe?

At times I saw Matthew. I smelt him, and the smoke of his cigarettes. I could hear his footsteps wandering the house. Was I hallucinating? Was I mad? If I voiced my feelings would I be locked up? This was a constant terror.

I was out more, but hated meeting people, because they didn't know what to say. Either they avoided me, and walked on eggshells around me, or, not knowing what to say they wouldn't give it much thought. One friend said, 'You'll be all right because mother nature kicks in, and you've got your other kids there.' That was true, but not very helpful. I felt like asking her which one of her children she could live without but managed to hold in the words. In truth, there *are* no words that will take away the pain, but if someone is genuine, they can't go too far wrong.

You would think that those working in the funeral business would always have the right words, but one of the women working in the memorial headstone masonry shop showed the utmost insensitivity.

I'd thought long and hard about the headstone, and what to have engraved on it. The thought of it kept me going in the weeks after the funeral. I was determined to find the perfect words. It was one thing I could do for my son. It gave me focus.

Finally, I had decided.

TRUESDALE

In loving memory of

MATTHEW JAMES

Sunrise 3rd April 1995

Sunset 11th October 2012

LOVED AND REMEMBERED EVERY DAY

I went in to check the spelling, and there was a woman on the desk I'd not seen there before. Hearing my name, she said, 'Oh, yes, that was the boy who took his own life, wasn't it? I remember. I was just about to go on my holidays.'

I looked at her, blankly, hoping she'd stop talking, but she continued. 'It looked like a really big funeral. I saw all the mourners, and there seemed to be a lot of young people.'

I nodded and pointed at the file on her desk. 'About the headstone,' I said. 'I've come in to do an amendment.'

'Yes,' She said, looking at me with wide eyes. 'But did *you* find him?' Your son?'

I looked at her in astonishment. 'I really can't talk about this now. I have to go out to the car. My children are there.'

'You have others? That's lucky. What do you have?'

'Two girls and a boy.' I stared at her, willing her to shut up.

'What ages are they? Oh!' She put her hand up her mouth. 'Did *they* find him?'

Her eyes were on stalks. She's really enjoying this, I thought. Here she is, working in the headstone business – dealing with bereaved families every day, and she has absolutely no empathy.

When I didn't answer, she said. 'Or, did they see him?'

Did this woman believe it was normal practice to ask such questions? Not even my friends, or relatives, has been so insensitive. 'I'm sorry,' I said. 'But I can't go there.'

It's different when a good friend asks questions. My friend, Amy, had supported me from day one. She had encouraged me to return to college and take a degree in youth work, and after Matthew's death she sent regular text messages encouraging me to meet up with her yet understanding if I felt unable to do so.

When, one day, I showed her into Matthew's room, she asked me how, exactly, he had died. I happily spoke to her about it, because she knew Matthew, and was affected by his death. I told her how I had found him, what he had done, and I told her that, from my research, I knew that he would have lost consciousness quickly, and then died. It was good to be able to talk about it and to someone so genuine, and, allowing her to understand was much better, for her, than keeping her at the mercy of her worst imaginings.

When two weeks had gone by, I decided to get the ironing done – anything, I thought, to occupy my mind. I was enjoying the peaceful rhythm of it, when, picking up a pair of jeans, I noticed they were Matthew's. His favourite pair. I dropped them, back into the basket in shock. And that was it. I unravelled.

Since Matthew's death my chest had hurt. It felt as if my heart was, literally, breaking. But at that moment, I felt I couldn't breathe. I wanted to be with Matthew, to know that he was ok. I couldn't take the pain anymore – and I thought I would end my life.

I remembered hearing of a boy, who had taken his life some years before. His father had set up a suicide prevention agency in Belfast, in his memory. I longed to know how he, the father, had kept living, and decided to ring the helpline to find out.

A woman answered the phone and asked how she could help.

'My son died two weeks ago,' I said, through my tears. 'It was suicide. I'm thinking of taking my own life.'

She asked me to tell her, exactly, how I was feeling and when I did so, she said, 'Yes. That's normal.'

'Normal?'

'Yes. It's natural to think life isn't worth living. It sounds like you could use some herbal bac remedies to calm you down. Can you come to Belfast to pick them up?'

I nearly dropped the phone in shock. 'My son is dead,' I said, again. 'I want to die too. Please can I talk to your founder? I want to know how he felt – how he got through.'

'We don't have government funding,' she said, failing, utterly, to answer my question. 'We rely on charitable donations, but the remedies will help.'

I don't know what I had been expecting, but it wasn't that. I imagined I would be helped, counselled, or at the very least, listened to. But I hadn't been heard. It took a lot to make me turn to them for help. A lot of desperation. And this was their advice? I just couldn't believe it.

One thing. Their lack of response had made me angry; and it was this anger that stopped me from killing myself. And I lived another day.

Support came from unexpected places. When the parents of Matthew's friends from early childhood, Corinna and Andy got in touch, I was surprised. I hadn't known Matthew had kept up with their sons James and Josh. Corrina's sister, Kelleigh was a support, too. Her frequent text messages always brightened my day. She understood my need to know where Matthew was.

'He's still around you,' she said. As a fervent Catholic she was convinced of it. I would have loved to believe her, and to have such a strong faith, but if she was right, why did I not have more of a sense of him?

Kritti told me to stop crying. She said, 'you are holding him back here. Let him go.'

Kritti is Hindu, and Karen believes in Angels. And as for my mum – through her Christian faith she believed that Matthew would be in Heaven, but her Buddhist background taught her that Matthew would be reborn and would stay around his body until after the funeral. Her words took me back to my grandmother's funeral in Singapore. She was cremated, but beforehand, monks had prayed over her body. We all offered her gifts – by burning money and clothes at the temple – and by offering food.

Gathering as a family, we stayed with my grandmother's body, praying. It was a hot day, yet there were no insects around – despite all the food on display. But when we sat, having a meal, I saw a particularly beautiful butterfly. 'Look!' I said, pointing it out to my auntie.

She smiled. 'Some people believe that is your grandmother, Sharon, come to join us.'

I loved that idea. It seemed so apt.

One friend, Joanne, visiting me a few weeks after Matthew had died told me that the devil had got into my house and taken Matthew. I was so shocked. For weeks, afterwards, I wandered around in a daze, wondering what I had done that was so wrong to let the devil into my house. Clearly, I was a bad mother – a bad person – who needed to be punished.

I went around the house like a woman possessed, anointing each doorway with oil. I repeated a prayer. 'God, please can you protect our home,' I chanted, then did the same for the car, the dog, and for Natasha's horse.

I believed that Matthew was in heaven – a place where there were no tears, no bullying and no girlfriend troubles – but I needed to be sure of it. When I was pregnant with Daniel it was a high-risk pregnancy. I had to have balloon therapy to treat irregular bleeding. The lining of my womb had burned away.

The doctors were worried. They said there were no guarantees that Daniel would be born. I googled the condition and was not reassured. I read of cases where pregnant women had miscarriages, or a haemorrhage.

Noticing my concern, Matthew said, 'What do they know? Just pray, Ma, and things will be ok'.

I wondered did Matthew pray. Did I teach him enough about God? I'd talked about God. I'd reminded Matthew to pray and I'd played religious and spiritual music. Was that enough?

And if it was, was it enough that Matthew believed in God? Would he have to ask for forgiveness? Had he done so? These thoughts turned into an obsession. I'd talk to Matthew in his room, and at the graveside and ask him. And I googled all these different sites, reading people's accounts of near-death experience. I envied the people who had experienced such things. I began to pray to God asking him to let me die for a few minutes, so that I could see Matthew just one more time.

After that one call to the suicide prevention agency, I didn't confide in anyone. I couldn't. Not really. But when Terry asked me how I was doing, I'd give him a sort of answer – a one liner. That was enough. If I said, 'I was at the grave all day,' he would hug me, but know that I wasn't keen to talk. When, during the worst times, I told him, 'I don't feel good,' or, 'I don't want to be here,' he would say, 'It's early days, Sharon. It's grief. And its normal.'

Normal. I began to hate that word. I know there are meant to be stages of grief, but nobody talks of the utter desperation. Wanting to die could *not* be normal. And there were still days when I contemplated suicide; it seemed the only way I could stop the pain; but something always stopped me.

I thought, if something happens to me, Annie Jean will be all right, because she can live with her dad, Mark. Daniel will be happy with Terry, but Natasha doesn't have anyone, because she hasn't a good relationship with James. I had to live for her.

9

Denial

Whilst I sleepwalked through my days, concentrating on simply getting through, I showed a brave face to the world. Not even my family guessed how I was feeling. My friends didn't either, yet they were the ones who knew how to help me. I don't know how. They seemed to know instinctively.

I liked that. Because when people ask, 'is there anything I can do,' they mean well. But the problem is that it's hard to ask for help – or to admit that you need it. Especially if you don't know what you need. It's one of my worst traits. And when I was in that place where I wasn't thinking logically, my real friends gave me glimpses of logic and of what normal life was.

Many people told me that I had lost weight, and that annoyed me. It's not as if I was trying to diet - I didn't care what I looked like and hadn't even realised that I was thinner. I never looked in the mirror because I couldn't stand seeing Matthew's eyes staring back at me. Good friends instinctively realised this and they didn't comment. They simply brought me a sandwich, making sure that I ate it.

Karen lives in Belfast; she has been my constant friend. She was there when I was going through my divorce – through all the bad times, and the good. She never tried to comfort me with her thoughts or opinions, but she let me talk. Acknowledging that, yes, I had lost Matthew, she let me say something about him fifty times a day if I needed to. She never changed the subject. She was never afraid to bring Matthew up in a conversation or share a memory of him. She knew this helped me, because I never stopped thinking about Matthew.

If, when she rang, I sounded especially low, she would say, 'Right, Sharon. I'm coming down.' She would drop everything, come to the house, and say, 'We're going for a cup of coffee.'

I might protest, and say I wasn't up to it, but she always won. She must have noticed that I wasn't in good form; that my hair needed combing and I hadn't slept – she must've known, but she never said it. And doing something so normal with her to protect me always made me feel better. And as I started to do more normal things, I was unknowingly beginning to break the bad habits I had gotten into. All that Googling to find out where Matthew was, all that feverish researching through the bible, all the days spent at the grave, in his room – all this gradually stopped.

Roberta lives further away, but she helped by keeping everything normal. She didn't change. We generally met about four times a year for birthdays, and though she increased the number of times she saw, me, the traditions we'd set up didn't change. At Christmas, for example, instead of buying us presents, she would get tickets for a show. And, like Karen, she allowed me to talk, or not to talk – whatever it was that I needed. I am so grateful to them both.

Seeing Roberta, though, was a reminder to me, that before Matthew died, I wasn't the best friend to her that I'd always thought I was. Years earlier when she lost her father, I attended the funeral, but that was it. I had no idea what death means and what she was going through. Did I offer her normality and an opportunity to talk? I really don't know, but I doubted I'd been as good a friend to her as she was now being to me, and I felt guilty.

They weren't the only ones to lend support. Matthew's friends, Gregory, Kenny, Ricky, Stuart and Richard began to appear now and then. That was a surprise. And they were brilliant! They wouldn't ask how they could help; they simply saw what needed doing. Recognising that our large garden needed attention, they just got on with it, and this wasn't just a once off – they kept it maintained.

Other friends of his helped too. James Nicholl brought over a bag of coal around the time of the funeral; Kelleigh asked me to go for coffee, and Darren came into his own, later, organising get togethers for Matthew's anniversaries.

His friends were sensitive to my feelings – displaying a wisdom beyond their years. They kept their distance, anxious not to intrude on my grief, and would wait until I asked them in, to have a cup of tea. I loved chatting to them about their nights out – and I loved the house being full of friendship and laughter again. It helped bring back memories of Matthew. I could, almost, believe that he was still alive. I loved checking out their Facebook updates, proud that they have grown into such lovely young men. Obviously, all this gave me a pang, too. Why wasn't Matthew there, with them? Why had he been taken?

Matthew was in my mind all the time, yet sometimes I would forget little details. Towards the end of the year I woke one morning in a panic. I couldn't remember which clothes we buried Matthew in. I rang a friend, Debbie and she said, 'He wore that red shirt, remember,' but I couldn't remember. She had to send me through a picture of Matthew wearing that shirt – one that appeared on Facebook.

If the adults who saw me around the town tended to avoid me, the young didn't. I'd be greeted by teenagers all the time. I didn't know all of them, but they knew me all right. They'd say, 'Your Matthew's Mum, aren't you?'

I'm particularly grateful to the young, because Matthew's death had hit them hard. I heard later, that many of Matthew's friends had needed counselling.

After a few weeks these strange rumours started circling. I don't know who was spreading them, but I could hardly believe it when Natasha stomped in one day, and in a fury, said, 'You know what people are saying, Ma?'

'Ma?' This gave me a pleasurable jolt. That was Matthew's name for me; Natasha always called me Mum.

'No,' I said, turning down the TV. 'What are people saying?'

'That Matthew didn't kill himself.' She flung herself down, beside me, on the sofa. 'They said he would never have done it. That he was always happy.'

I looked at her, open mouthed, thinking of the times he had tried before; thinking of all his problems. 'I suppose they only saw one side of Matthew,' I said, cautiously. 'The fun loving, party going popular side. The Matthew everyone loved.'

'Yeah, right.'

'So how did he die then? What are they saying?'

'You won't believe it,' she said, flicking her eyes upwards. 'They're saying that he fell out with his friends.'

'Oh. And?'

'And that they murdered him. I know!' she said, seeing my shocked expression. 'I told you you wouldn't believe it.'

'Surely nobody believes that?' I said. 'They couldn't.'

'Yeah, well other people are saying that he did kill himself – but only because he was as high as a kite and didn't know what he was doing. But he wasn't, Ma. Was he?'

I shook my head. 'Poor Matthew,' I said. 'Life just got too much for him. And no, he wasn't high. Far from it. He was scared and troubled.'

As I said this, I wondered, for the hundredth time, why Matthew hadn't confided in me. He knows my door is open to him 24 hours a day, yet he'd stayed away. Come to that, why hadn't I gone to him?

It was a question Mum posed every time I saw her. She had taken the death very badly. She never left the house. She lay on her sofa, all day, crying. Matthew had been her boy. She'd say, 'I loved him more than my own son.' And she wasn't averse to telling me that it was my fault. 'You were there,' she said, time and again. 'You could have done something.'

The terrible thing was, that I believed she might be right. Why hadn't I realised how bad he was feeling? I didn't need Mum to remind me. The guilt was already eating me up.

When Mum wasn't sounding off at me, she was having a rant about Shanice or Bronagh. And she wasn't the only one to hold Shanice to blame. Matthew's friends, grieving themselves, embraced Bronagh after Matthew's death. She, after all, was carrying his child. But Shanice had become an outcast. If she wandered into a pub all Matthew's friends walked out. It broke my heart.

'Shanice is grieving too,' I told them, the next time they came around to see how I was. 'It doesn't matter what you, or I think. Matthew loved Shanice, and he wouldn't want her treated that way.' I started to tell them about forgiveness and love and kindness

Some of Matthew's friends really *surprised* me. Take Jordan, the boy who'd ransacked the garage with Matthew. I often blamed him for being a bad influence, but I could now see him as a vulnerable young boy who missed his friend.

He got a large tattoo on his back to remember Matthew by, and he started attending church. It's as if Matthew's death has given him a purposeful life, and that thought brings me deep joy.

I have always loved Christmas. It's such a great excuse for a family get together, and that has always been my thing. As a child, I always dreamed of being part of a large close family – like the Walton's. After Matthews death this changed. The thought of spending the approaching Christmas season at home, without Matthew, was too hard to bear. Each year, when we'd decorated the tree, it would be Matthew, as the man of the house, to put the star on the top of the tree. I kept remembering the previous year, his face lit up by the fairy lights as we admired our handywork. How could we get through the holiday without him?

Before Matthew's death, Terry had suggested we should go away. I'd had pressures at work, and a break, we both decided, was just what I needed. And now, this seemed more relevant. 'It'll do you good,' Terry said. 'Nobody will know us, so there won't be any stupid questions or comments.'

Deciding on Lanzarote for some winter sun, we packed silly Santa things, and wrapped presents for each other. But on the day, we couldn't find a restaurant that sold Christmas dinner. So instead of it being a break for me, I ended up cooking dinner just as I always do. And I'm not the greatest cook.

The whole holiday was awful. You can leave home behind, but your grief comes along with you, as excess baggage. I couldn't sleep. Since Matthew's death I had avoided looking into a mirror, but that week, it seemed, I couldn't avoid it. There were mirrors everywhere! I'd catch of myself, and my eyes – Matthew's eyes – seemed to follow me around.

That really scared me. It wasn't just that I barely recognised the bony person I had become, with those sunken black eyes of grief - It brought me straight back to that moment that I found Matthew, staring at me in death. I still can't look at myself properly. Perhaps I never will be able to again.

'This holiday is doing you absolutely no good,' said Terry, when, waking and finding my side of the bed empty, he found me pacing the apartment in the dead of night. 'Let's cut it short. Let's just go home.'

I was tempted, but then realised I wouldn't sleep at home, either. So, we stayed. But I couldn't settle. I needed to be at Matthew's grave.

In January I started back to work. Terry was worried that I'd returned too soon, but once I arrived at EOTAS (Education other than at School), it was as if I was a different person. As a youth worker, I compliment curriculum subjects by delivering personal and social development programmes. This was the Prince's Trust Achieve Scheme and included a selection of preventative programmes based on the needs of the young people. The work suited me because I have a natural empathy with teenagers.

I'm good at my job. My employers have told me so, and so have the young people. They called me a rocket and a Melter, because I was always smiling and greeting them in the morning. If they weren't feeling the best, they knew they could always come to my room for a chat. They did well in their courses too; achieving 2 GCSE grade Bs from my subjects. At work I was organised, creative, flexible and passionate, but when I went home, in that first year, those skills switched off. It was as if I was two different people.

I'd worried about returning to work, not that it was too soon, but that things were so different. Supposing if, after Matthew's death, I found it harder to reach out to the teenagers? Would my grief affect that ability? Thankfully, it seemed not. They came in to see me, in groups, or individually, and we sat on comfy red chairs. They'd sit there and talk about everything and nothing, and their secrets came pouring out. I got a bit of a reputation. One lad, coming to me for the first time, said he didn't want to sit down. 'I'd rather stand,' he said.

'Oh?' I looked up at him in surprise. 'The chairs are really comfortable,' I patted a chair for emphasis.

'It's not that,' he said, shifting from foot to foot.

'What then?' I was intrigued.

'It's just, well, I've been warned,' he said, carefully avoiding my eye.

'Warned?'

'I was told, "Don't sit on a red chair, because, I don't know how Sharon does it, but as soon as you sit on a red chair you will start to talk."'

'That's good, isn't it?'

He blushed, confused. 'Yeah? But about *everything*.'

I had to laugh, looking at his expression of terror. But he *did* sit down, and he *did* talk about nothing and everything, just like everyone else.

The weird thing is, that I got the reputation amongst the kids for being, always happy. 'Why are you always smiling?' They'd say. They didn't know about Matthew, and I thought, gosh, I must really be a good actress.

The staff I worked with or came into contact with didn't comment on my weight loss, or the dark rings round my eyes, and they avoided the subject of Matthew. Like so many others, I think they were afraid of my reaction.

If they did mention him, it would be to say, 'He's in a better place now.' Or, 'You have to get on with your life – it's what Matthew would have wanted.' However, a colleague Mervyn, was different. He would ask how I was and would actively listen. He gave me the space to talk about my son, and that made a huge difference. On anniversaries or birthdays when I went into work, I was able to confide to him, and understanding my grief, he'd sit me down and bring me a cup of coffee.

I didn't talk to the students about Matthew – it didn't seem appropriate – until another colleague, Deneen, told me that one of the students had talked of him. 'He heard about your loss and would like to talk to you about Matthew. He says he doesn't know how to.'

At first, I recoiled from the idea, but I thought about it further, and agreed that I'd be happy to talk to him and discuss the mental health issues that teenagers like Matthew have – and depression and suicide in general. And we did talk. Word spread. Other students came to me too. Maybe a friend had taken their life or attempted to. I was able to talk about it in a rational way, and I hope I helped many of them to realise the hurt any suicide brings.

After that I noticed that I became a magnet for young people, and adults, who wished to talk about suicide. I didn't have to mention Matthew – or my experience – and they didn't know of it. But they seemed to pick up on a hidden, underlying sixth sense.

I liked my colleague, Deneen, and respected her too. She, Mervyn and I had the highest attendees and achievers amongst our students. We were a great team! We called ourselves the three musketeers.

But whilst work was going well, and I was able to help the students in my care, no supports were put in place to help me. My loss was virtually ignored. I didn't take days off for anniversaries for fear of letting staff and young people down at a time staff resources were scarce due to budgets. I did, sometimes, voice my need for time off – but support was not there. I was living as two people in a vicious circle where I'd leave Annie Jean to school and put my Christian CD on in the car. I'd have a word with God and I'd cry. I'd cry all the way into work – a journey that took 35 to 40 minutes. Then, when I arrived at work, I'd wipe my tears. When I left work, the same thing happened. I'd cry until I reached home, then I'd become Mum.

Terry could read me. He seemed to know, instinctively what I was feeling. His way to help me was to look after Daniel. Night times were the worst. That's when I felt scared. I couldn't close my eyes because that's when I saw Matthew, staring at me.

On 3rd February 2012, Bronagh's baby, Tyler Matthew Truesdale Gallagher came into the world. He was beautiful – the spitting image of his father, with swarthy skin and dark eyes. I can't count the number of people, who, seeing this, said what a comfort he must be to me, that it must be like having my own piece of Matthew.

And Tyler *is* a blessing. Of course, he is, but it's wrong to think of him as a replacement for Matthew. He's his own wee person with his own identity. Of all people, with the work I do, I'm aware of the importance of accepting everyone as themselves.

I dreaded Valentine's Day. It brought back such memories. Matthew loved it, but the date always seemed to take him by surprise. I'd get a panicked text from him when he was at work, saying, 'Could you pick up some flowers, or maybe chocolates?'

When the day came, I wanted to be near Matthew, and I went to his grave. I don't know why that day should be harder than any of the others, but it was. I was distraught! I was in such a state of despair, that I crouched down, on my hunkers, and started to scrabble in the earth. Screaming, out of control, I tried to dig him up, with my bare hands. It sounds crazy, and I think, for a minute, I had lost my mind.

I don't know what would have happened had a car not approached, but the sound of the engine brought me to my senses. I looked, in shock at the mud on my hands – the soil deeply ingrained in my nails. As I rubbed my hands together, trying to rid them of the worst muck, and began to tidy up the grave, I felt the weight of sadness. I sobbed until my chest hurt. Then, eventually, I rose to my feet, wiped my hands on my jeans, and walked towards my car blinded by tears.

If Valentine's day was bad, Mother's Day was worse. My mum bought the girls a card for me, and they signed it, and included Matthews name. That was such a lovely gesture, and I valued it – but even more precious was the card I found that Matthew had made me the year before. He'd written, 'To Ma. Happy Mother's Day, love Matt.' Simple words but now priceless.

I don't know why I chose that day to clear Matthew's room. But it felt like the time to sort his clothes ready to give to charity. Crying, as I sorted through his T-shirts and jeans, I planned where I would take them. I'd travel to towns a distance away, I decided, because how would I feel if I bumped into someone in Randalstown wearing my dead son's clothes? It didn't bear thinking about.

I did this task for the best of reasons; I felt the girls would cope better if these signs of their brother's existence were removed, but in retrospect, it was the worst thing I could possibly have done. I've regretted it many times since. And the act of doing it brought me to a low, dark place.

I fetched the tablets I'd found in Matthew's room a fortnight after the funeral and had decided to keep them. Looking at them, with desperation in my heart, I thought how easy it would be to take them, and to end it all. I poured myself a glass of water and put the tablets in my hand. I was crying. Tempted. So tempted, because then, I was as convinced that I would see Matthew again as this pain in my chest would leave me

Thinking of our meeting in heaven, turned my mind to God – the God I prayed to. I collected my bible and stood on it. Then I began to talk to God. I said, 'Blessed are those who mourn, but I do not feel comforted, your word says I can find rest with Jesus, but I am exhausted. Your words promised you would make my pain better, and you've let me down.' I don't know how long I stood there. Minutes? Half an hour? But eventually, exhausted from all the crying, I walked into the en-suite and threw the tablets down the toilet and flushed it. I lived for another day as I took out my bible and stood on it praying 'father I put my trust in you I am standing on your every word, please help me'

10

Crashing

One night, after months of sleeplessness I bought myself a mini bottle of Baileys. I drank it, and it took the edge off my grief. It helped me sleep that first night, so I bought another bottle. After a while, though, one mini bottle wasn't enough, and a litre bottle of Baileys became part of a weekly shop.

Sometimes, two glasses didn't seem enough, and I'd drink a third. Once or twice I'd go for a fourth. That's really out of character for me – I've never enjoyed alcohol, but if that's what it took to help me sleep and be able to cope at home and at work, then, I reasoned, it was fair enough. And the months went on – with my weekly shopping increased to a litre bottle of Baileys and Tia Maria.

On a bright spring day, I arrived at Matthew's grave, and an older man approached me. He worked there, and he asked me who had I can come to see. I said, 'I'm here to see my son. He took his own life.'

He said he was sorry for my loss, and we chatted for a while, then he told me that his son had taken *his* own life too. 'I didn't see the signs,' he said, clearly distressed. 'Did you? Did you see the signs?'

I thought about it. 'Well,' I said. 'Matthew did say to me, 'I'm not living to an old age. That's why I'm living such a full life now. I did find that strange,' I said. 'I asked him what he meant, and he just shrugged, and said he just knew it.'

The man listened, deep in thought. He said, again, that he hadn't seen any signs. That his son's death had come like a bolt from the blue. As I drove home, I thought about that. And wondered if that would be worse – if the lack of signs would leave you even more in shock.

103 | P a g e

A few months later I saw that man again. I'd gone to the sink by the toilets to get some water for flowers, and there he was. But something had happened to him. When he greeted me, he slurred his words. He looked scruffy, and clearly hadn't washed. He looked me up and down, taking in my face, brightened by makeup, my crisp shirt and freshly washed jeans.

'How do you always look so good?' he said, perhaps in acknowledgment of his own state. He seemed to expect an answer, so I said, 'You know, and I know, that when I put on this makeup, I am trying to hide something.'

He nodded, but I doubt he really understood. But when I'm feeling really bad, make-up helps me to hide my grief. When the comic actor, Robin Williams died, people were amazed to hear that this funny man had been in such a deep depression, that his life became unbearable. And though I felt shocked at the time, having laughed so hard at all his movies, I understood. Having lived through grief I know that, sometimes, the worse you feel, the more you try and convince the world that everything is okay.

We were both quiet for a minute. Then the man said, 'Are you ever tempted to turn to the drink?'

I stared, and blushed, wondering if he could read my mind.

'If you have, my dear,' he continued, 'My advice, is, don't!'

I took that to heart, and, in a way, that man saved me. I stopped. I do have the odd drink, at parties or to celebrate, but I've never been tempted to use it to block out pain. Never again.

The problem was, that I transferred my dependence on Baileys to other addictions. Oh, I didn't take drugs – I would never do that, and not just because I saw the negative effect cannabis had on Matthew. In May, I got myself a new phone, and I discovered an app for eBay auction. Intrigued, I clicked on it, and the phone started to tell me that I had won certain items and lost others. It was intriguing!

Parcels started to arrive for me, and they kept on coming! I won a box of spatulas that I have no memory of bidding for; then a pair of riding boots arrived. They made more sense; I'd clearly bought them for Natasha; except that she's a size five and the boots were size eight!

This went on for months. There were so many deliveries that I couldn't keep up. I never even opened some of the boxes. When Natasha saw me scowl one day, because I hadn't won the 30 bicycle helmets I'd bid on, she took me in hand, and said it had to stop.

She got rid of the app. 'It's crazy,' she said. 'It's costing you so much money.' She then helped me sell on all the stuff I had accumulated.

I was grateful to her, but I missed the buzz of it all. Bidding had helped me to pass those endless night-time hours. And it had given me the illusion of control. Looking for something else to do in those lonely, frightening small hours, I came across the game, Candy Crush. Yes, it was another addiction, but as Natasha pointed out, at least it was one that came without financial cost.

There were good moments during this time, and kindness came from unexpected sources. One morning washing up at the sink I looked up and found myself smiling. Wilma and her husband Paul had arrived the previous day with two hanging baskets full of flowers which they placed on Matthews bedroom entrance. And what's more, they maintained the baskets for me. That gesture helped me at a dark time. It was a special gift with which to remember Matthew.

It was hard, as a youth worker, to admit that I needed outside help. Terry had suggested, many times, that I should go to a grief support group for those who had suffered a loss by suicide, and in September, I decided to comply. There were maybe eight sets of parents there, and one had lost his son in recent weeks.

Clearly it helped many people; there was one man there who had lost his son 12 years previously. He wrote poems to help him cope, but he did most of the talking. He had survived his loss, and the meetings had helped in this, but I wanted more instant help. The meeting didn't move on from him, and I went home feeling it had been a waste of time. Did my failure to act as he did indicate that I was mad?

I tried it again. And the next time a young girl was delivering an art session. I cooperated with her, but more to help her facilitate the class. I tried it once more. That time, it was a busy session, but everyone was at a different stage of grief. One parent, whose child had died five years before, told another, who had suffered loss just weeks before, that grief gets better over time. That parent took offence, and a row broke out. I didn't go back again. It's brilliant for many people; I know that; but at that time in my cycle of grief, it simply wasn't for me.

I struggled on. I got through Matthews first anniversary, and woke the following day, a Saturday pleased that I had survived a whole year without him. But later, my sister rang in a state of shock. She'd been into the butchers, but as she'd picked up her meat, the entire counter crashed on her feet, breaking them. She was unable to walk for weeks.

The following day Mum was taken into hospital. She was having tests, and I was frantic with worry. I was driving to college on Tuesday, minding my own business when there was this horrendous bang, and I was jolted forwards. I'd driven slap bang into a red van which was covered with white graphics. I sat there, rigid with shock, and when the driver climbed out of the van, and came over to me, I waited, anxiously for him to shout abuse. He didn't.

'I didn't see the van,' I said, apologising over and over again. 'How *could* I not have seen it?'

'Don't be panicking,' he said, brushing away my apologies. 'Are you okay?'

'I think so,' I said, wiggling my toes, and shrugging my shoulders. 'Nothing seems to hurt.'

'That's all that matters,' he said. He was quiet as he helped me out of the car. I stumbled out, trying to hide my tears. If he noticed them, he didn't comment. But once we had both established that I hadn't any cuts or broken bones, he sighed with relief. Then he said, quietly, 'My best friend was killed last week.'

I looked up at him in horror, and instinctively put my hand on his arm. 'I am so sorry,' I said. 'And here am I, adding to your troubles.'

My car wasn't the only thing to crash that day. My whole system did too. I don't remember ringing for help – but I must have, because my sister picked me up, and drove me to her house. I was sitting there, still shaking and crying, when Terry arrived to take me home.

He hugged me, voicing his relief that I was unharmed, then he said, 'I'm glad this happened.'

I looked at him in horror.

'You're okay,' he said. 'The van driver is okay. Something had to make you stop.'

'What do you mean?'

'Look at you,' he said. 'You're not eating. You're not sleeping. You've lost so much weight – go on like this, you'll be a skeleton. Something had to give.'

He was right. That man, driving the big red van made me stop and evaluate myself. It might sound fanciful, but I believe he was sent by my guardian angel. Later, he rang me. I was. I assumed he wanted to know about the insurance, and told him not to worry, that it was all in hand, but no. 'I just wanted to make sure that you're okay,' he said. That meant so much.

And of course, I wasn't all right. By some miracle I wasn't physically hurt, but afterwards, I had a sort of mini breakdown. It was as if my whole body froze. I couldn't go to work, I couldn't even think straight, so I made an appointment with the doctor. I told him what had been happening, and he suggested that I take an anti-depressant.

'Have I got depression then?' I asked. 'Is that what this is?'

He didn't answer me; not directly. 'There's a lot going on in your life, and these tablets will help – the main thing is that they will help you sleep,' he said, telling me I should continue to take them for the next six months. I started taking the pills, and I began to manage. I still felt sad. I still missed Matthew every minute of every day, but I knew I would get through.

I often wonder, was I depressed? I was never diagnosed as such, and it was not a word I related to. When I learned all about PTSD – Post Traumatic Stress Disorder – the term seemed more relatable. Because finding Matthew had been, without doubt, the most traumatic thing I have ever experienced. I wouldn't wish something like that on anybody.

Then I went for counselling – something I had never thought I would need. Certainly, the old Sharon had never done so. When I told the counsellor why I was there, she said, 'Looking at you, I can't believe you have been through all that.'

I was a little taken aback, and, seeing this, she said, 'I shouldn't have said that. It was judgemental of me.'

I liked her for that. For being so honest. She then asked me what I wanted her to do for me. 'I don't really know,' I said, matching her honesty. 'But I know what I *don't* want you to do.'

She looked puzzled.

'I don't want you to regurgitate every book I've just been reading.'

She laughed, and to my relief, she never fell into that trap. I'm not sure, really, what she did, but I left, after that first session feeling that a weight had been lifted. And that night, I slept well for the first time in weeks. I went back the following week, and the third. And *that* week, when I was telling her all about Matthew's last night, and my guilt for not realising how low he was, she interrupted me.

'Sharon,' she said. 'You said to me that your bedroom door was always open.'

'That's right.' I was impressed that she remembered. She wasn't taking notes.

'So, Matthew – and your other children – can come in an any time of day?'

'Or night. Yes.'

'In that case, Matthew decided, on that night, not to come to you.'

'You mean...'

'It wasn't your fault, Sharon. You *were* there for him.'

I looked at her, in silence, thinking to myself, she really does listen. This woman is really very good.

'We can't control other people, Sharon,' she said, quietly. 'In the end, they make their own choices.'

Digesting her words, I thought back to Matthew, and to all the things he had said. Like, 'I'm not going to live until I am old.' Was he thinking, in his head, that he would have an accident? Or did he mean that he planned to end his life? I don't know, but he said things like that more and more as he went through his teens. He always said, 'I don't see myself as an old man.'

After nine months I stopped talking about Matthew in the present tense, as if he was still alive, and finally, accepted that he was dead. Matthew was dead. Until then, I'd half expected him to appear and say, 'Ma, it was just a dream.'

I went to that counsellor for about nine months, and she helped, she really did. Knowing that I worked in the same general area, she treated me with respect. She'd listen, always, but she also discussed the latest research with me. She'd say, 'Have you read this, Sharon,' or, 'have you heard about this?' She was genuine. That's why I kept going back.

During that time, I decided to take a counselling course, and I applied for a part-time course at the Northern Regional College in partnership with university of Ulster. As part of the training, we had to tell a story to the rest of the class about an incident in our lives that had had an impact on us.

I decided to talk about my dad; I'd say he and my mum split up when I was ten years old, and how awful that was. It ticked the box and I thought it would be easy. After all, I didn't have any particular feelings for my dad.

Then I listened to the stories that the others told. One girl had lost a parent through suicide; another had been abused by her mother. I looked at those people and thought, oh my gosh! I would never have guessed such terrible things had happened to you. You seem so strong.

They were all being so real; so truthful. How could I go up there and tell the sob story about my father, when that was not the issue that haunted me? I'd signed up for this course and agreed that I would be truthful in the classroom. Yet I didn't feel able to talk about Matthew. It was too raw.

I stood up and walked to the front of the classroom. I took out my notes and started to read. 'When I was ten years old my dad left,' I said. Then I looked up and saw all those trusting eyes looking at me. I folded up my notes and tucked them under my arm.

'I'll be honest with you,' I said. 'I was going to talk about my dad, and how hard it all was, but there is something else I really want to share.' There was a flip-chart paper on a stand. I wrote then pointed to the date Matthew died, and said, 'This is the date that the real Sharon Truesdale died, and the new Sharon Truesdale was born.' The class looked troubled.

'The reason for this,' I said, 'is that my son, Matthew, took his own life.' I don't know what else I said, but I remember I cried. And when I looked up, I noticed that everyone in the room had tears in their eyes. I thought, why are they crying? It's my son.'

This exercise, all about self-reflection, helped us to become more self-aware. This was the start of my healthy grieving - learning to apply everything I was learning and easily whilst practicing with others; unconditional positive regard, being genuine, non-judgemental came naturally, when talking to others in the class, as they were showing me the same; the real learning was applying this to myself.

It taught me to listen to myself, not be so hard on myself and more importantly to take care of myself. It's like when you're on an aeroplane and they tell you put your own oxygen mask on before helping anyone else. How ridiculous this sounded to me when I first heard it, surely as a mother my reaction would be to put the mask onto my children. Without taking care of me first, I would not be able to look after my children. This was a turning point in my new life.

We were taught the importance of living in the here and now, rather than harking back to the past, or fretting about the future. This takes practice and nearly 6 years on I still need to practice using Mindfulness Techniques.

Another lesson was a reminder that we don't have control over other people. That's important when you are counselling people. It's a rule that is easy to say, but not so easy to believe. I learned that on the course and I learned it from Matthew.

In many ways the counselling course was as useful to me as going to counselling had been. It took me to places I would have happily avoided. Through that course I made sense of the stages of the grieving process.

I'd heard of the stages before, but now I had to learn to apply them by making sense of all that was happening to me. I had to be honest about my thoughts and feelings; and even embrace them as they came. Then, I learned, I could start to truly grieve, and work towards finding some sort of acceptance. Only then could I move on to live a healthy life, and to ask for support and help when I needed it. Ultimately, I needed to accept Matthew's death, think about it without guilt, and live my own life.

Around that time, in the February, I turned forty. Whenever, in the past, I'd thought of that particular milestone I'd remember that, by then, Matthew would be eighteen. 'We'll go out on my birthday and get our first drink together,' I always told him. Now that the day was here, Matthew's absence created a yawning gap. Nobody knew what to do.

The family were good. They arranged a dinner for us all at a local restaurant, and I bought a lovely dress from a charity shop in Barnardo's, Belfast. We went through the motions and did what was expected. They bought me presents and ordered a cake for dessert. They all sang 'Happy Birthday,' and I blew out the candle. We acted as if we were happy, but we were just going through the motions. We were all, acutely, aware that an important family member wasn't there.

11

Coping

From the time of Matthew's death, there were things that happened that were difficult to explain. There was the bird, on that first day – the one that I saw in Matthew's room, which flew out through a small gap, as if by instinct. There were two pigeons around at significant times – and there was the smell of cigarette smoke in the house when I was alone.

Two days after Matthew died, I had a dream. There were three women in my room, looking down at me. One of them looked like my father's mum, Annie. She was wearing an old fashioned long, vyella night dress. She was kissing my hand, and although I couldn't see Matthew, I was aware that he was standing behind the women. The dream was so vivid. It was almost as if I was awake. I actually felt the softness of that kiss on my hand.

I've always attended church quite regularly, but after Matthew died, I realised I should make a point of attending in order to hold onto my faith. I went every week, and it gave me comfort. At every service, I would gain some peace. I tried different religions. My dad was a Presbyterian, so I sampled that. I tried evangelism, and I tried the Baptist church. But that one was a bit too strict for me.

God was there for me when I was growing up, and now I needed him more than ever. I attended Victory Praise and prayed daily. 'Father, I know it is written that there is a plan. I trust you, and I stand on your every word. Father, I know that you will help me through this.'

For all that, I went through moments of doubt; moments of thinking that God didn't understand what I was going through. But nine months after Matthew's death, sitting in church with the sun streaming through the stained-glass windows, I remembered that God had a son who died too. So of course, he *did* understand.

When I was at my worst, on the verge of a breakdown, Kritti invited me to her house for a few days. Kritti is like a sister to me and I know that I can get to her house and be kept safe. When I explained all this to Karen, and told her that I needed to get away, Karen said she would take time off work and would come along too. I was delighted, but shocked. Karen is always so busy and committed to her work.

'And while we're there, we can go to a fortune teller,' she said. 'I'd like to be there when you hear from Matthew.'

'What are you on about?' I was flummoxed.

'I think you'll hear from Matthew,' she said, 'and that will give you a sense of peace.'

I'm normally sceptical of such things, but Karen believes in angels, and the books she had bought for me on angels *had* given me comfort. I'd accompanied Karen when she went to Belfast to hear the writer, Lorna Byrne, who sees angels, and believes they are all around us, and I could see how fervently people believe in them. Karen had also got me the box set of 'Ghost Whisperer.' Watching it, I was able to imagine that Matthew was standing beside me. The image was so vivid. He was telling me that he loves me, and that he wants me to strive for the job of my dreams but more importantly he wanted me to live and not barely exist.

But I wasn't putting too much faith into this visit to a fortune teller. I'd been to see them before. Well, hasn't everybody? But that was when we were at college and wanted to know about boyfriends and holidays. It was all a bit of fun. This was different. Did I really need a fortune teller to tell me where Matthew was? I felt I already knew.

'Matthew is in heaven,' I told Karen. 'I'm convinced of it. So, what's the point of all this?'

I was fighting a losing battle. When Karen gets her teeth into something, she's hard to dissuade. And her enthusiasm won out. I decided to give it a go and for what Karen would call fate the following morning when we arrived, we phoned a fortune teller and got 3 appointments for that morning.

When we arrived, the woman took us into this healing room. She put me in a gloriously comfortable chair and gave me what looked like was some dumbbells wrapped with copper wiring. Then she took us through some breathing exercises. It was supposed to relax us, but I found it hard to concentrate, and I started laughing hysterically. I found that I couldn't stop, and the healer did not appreciate this.

She looked at me, sharply. 'You think I talk shit? You think I'm stupid?' She was, clearly upset, but this just made me laugh more. Kritti and Karen were mortified. 'She's just nervous,' said Karen. 'Sharon always laughs when she's nervous.'

Well, when I got into her room for my private consultation, my gosh I wasn't laughing. It takes a lot to scare me, but she terrified me with her knowledge. Without saying anything she told me that it was Matthew's anniversary the next week; she told me how he had died; she talked about the argument between the two girls, and whenever she spoke to me, she referred to me as, 'Ma.' How did she guess that that is what Matthew always called me? How would she know?

'When you found your son, there was a bird in the room,' she said. 'And you know that cupboard? The one in the kitchen where Matthew used to keep his protein shakes? Often you find that open. Is that right?'

I nodded, wordless. It was true. The cupboard had a stiff door – one that was hard to open because layers of paint had made it a tight fit. And I had, indeed found it open, many, many times. It had always puzzled me.

'That's Matthew trying to contact you,' she said. 'He's trying to show you that he's okay.'

She was quiet for a while, apparently going into a trance, then she spoke again.

'Matthew is worried about you,' she said. 'He thinks you might feel bereft on Mother's Day. He says you're to buy yourself some flowers – as a gift from him.' She smiled. 'He says, 'nothing too expensive. He's thinking of some daffodil bulbs in a pot.'

Then she laughed. 'To be honest, Sharon, from the sense I'm getting of your Matthew, I suspect he'd have just lifted some flowers from somebody's garden.' And how right she was! For all that, a part of me remained sceptical. The whole scenario was too reminiscent of the movie, Ghost with Whoopee Goldberg – and the way the fortune teller took on Matthew's personality freaked me out.

For all that, it gave me comfort to know that Matthew was okay. And when she passed on his messages, I felt real comfort. 'He says, I love you Ma, and I'm sorry that my death made you suffer.' Since meeting that fortune teller, I feel sure that Matthew is with me. How else could she have known about the strange things that had happened in the house?

Returning home, I felt calmer. I can't explain some of those odd experiences, but at least I now know I'm not mad! I still live by my faith in God, but I am now more open to these alternative forms of belief.

12

Fighting

I will never forget Matthew. I don't want others to forget him either. I want his legacy to be of some use. I don't want anyone else to have to go through the pain I experienced, and I want his death to help other people, and to make them think before taking their lives. This is why I searched so hard for answers.

All through Matthew's troubled life, I had been looking for help. From his times of trauma – witnessing the domestic violence and hurting because contact with his father was so spasmodic. I looked for help when he was being bullied at school; when he experimented with drugs; and when he found himself in trouble with the law. I knew he needed professional help and did everything in my power to secure it for him.

There are, officially, processes in place to safeguard and support a young person with their mental health difficulties, but in the ten years – from when Matthew was seven until his death, I sought help for Matthew. He was referred to Social Services 17 times, but we could never get our foot through the door.

This lack of support was especially worrying during Matthew's last year of life. There were so many distressing signs; his self-harm, and his earlier attempts to end his life. We looked for help and kept on looking. Terry and I have training – and we put into place all the possible safeguards at home, but we were well aware that Matthew needed outside help. That's why we went to our GP and to CAMHS.

I could never understand why they had been unable to offer Matthew the support he so badly needed, and in the months following his death, I made a complaint to the Northern Health Trust about CAMHS. The head psychiatrist and head social worker took my complaint seriously; they came to see me the month after Matthew died. I remember it so well. The two of them sitting opposite me, on the sofa, drinking tea.

I reiterated that I'd warned CAMHS of the state that Matthew was in. I'd told them about the attempts he's taken on his life, and of my worries that without expert intervention he would complete suicide, and the head psychiatrist put up his hands in mock-surrender.

'I'm sorry,' he said. 'On this occasion the trust failed you and it failed Matthew.' Then, shaking his head slightly, he added, 'If I had been there, things would have been different.'

I was happy with that. If they could accept that my complaint was valid, I reasoned, the procedures would be tightened up in the future.

At that time, I believed that Matthew was the only young boy to have been so badly let down, and that ours was the only family to have been denied the help we needed. I thought it was a once off. But that, I discovered, wasn't true. And if young people were not getting the support from professionals; if parents weren't getting appropriate information, how would the situation ever improve? The services need to change because suicide is on the increase. It's not good enough that policies are put into drawers and forgotten about as the aims and objectives for their existence are not met and inequalities creep in where they pick and choose who to help.

When the head social worker made her report the following January, she highlighted the deficiencies in social services. In many ways it was a wonderful, thorough report. But she rowed back on what was said at the meeting at my house. Whilst saying that social services had let us down over the years, she failed to address her own part in this. My question had been, why did CAMHS not help Matthew, and the report didn't address that.

When CAMHS said that they were not aware of Matthew's history, and didn't know he had tried to take his own life, I couldn't accept it. Because both he and I told them that in

May, when we were there. It was made quite clear. It felt, to me, as if they were conspiring against me. And when I asked for a copy of all their records, it showed me that actually they did know that. Were they deliberately lying?

I'm not saying Matthew's death was their fault – but they took away a chance of helping him because without intervention he would succeed. That's what upset me so much.

The emails pinged backwards and forwards for two years. In a way, they kept me alive. There was nobody else who was going to fight for Matthew. It was up to me, and this was the one last thing I could do for him. I wasn't looking for money; I wanted change for someone else. My message was, 'follow your policies and procedures. And if you can't do that signpost the young person.' Because we didn't get that.

The letter I received from the head psychiatrist did not answer all the questions. At his conclusion he did apologise – but not for the inadequacies. He said he was sorry that I had been treated as a working colleague, rather than as a mother concerned for her son. But if that is how they viewed me, why could they not take on board my professional opinion that Matthew, as a young person, needed specialised help – and needed it urgently?

There was one issue which particularly angered me. I requested all the notes from CAMHS, in a desperate search for answers, and I wasn't one bit happy with the account I read. And worse, they were so dismissive of me. There was little empathy for me; little recognition that I was a grieving mother who was struggling to cope with her loss.

I was learning the stages of grief the hard way – and I assume, through their training, these specialist workers in CAMHS could recognise the stages in me. It seemed to me that they did so and were using my grief against me. They were making out that I hadn't told them about Matthew's previous attempts on his life; they said had they known they would have done things differently. It was as if they were trying to make me feel guilty.

And believe me, I felt guilty enough without their input. But the constant reports made me believe that I wasn't a good mother or a good youth worker. If I couldn't help my own son, how could I help others?

Yet I knew, logically, that Matthew completed suicide because they failed to offer him any intervention. When I asked why, the social worker said it was because they had failed to look at Matthew's history. And his history, surely, mattered? All the things that happened to Matthew – the violence he suffered at the hands of his father – the effects of the divorce – the bullying at school – the trouble with the police, and charge of rape – not to mention the times he voiced his wish that he were dead did this truly matter? Was it not enough to say, 'I asked my doctor for a lethal injection, my mum caught me with her dressing gown belt around my neck and struggled to get it off?'

Their lack of response really mattered to me. Changes were needed. It was too late for Matthew, but not for others. The rate of suicide in my hometown was increasing, and yet these experts did not do what they were supposed to. I said that, if I wasn't happy with the report, I would go public, and I meant every word!

At one stage, seeking another response, I showed Matthew's medical file to a lady who works with the Public Health Agency. I showed her the first page. It stated that Matthew had asked for a lethal injection from his GP, and that he continually stated that life wasn't worth living. I asked her what, presented with such a case she would expect to be done?

'First, the service would make sure the young person was safe,' she said, indicating that a plan would be drawn up for him. 'It could be a mixture of counselling, psychiatric treatment and medication.'

'Would it be sufficient to ask his mother to deliver an anger management programme?' I asked, adding that that was the only help offered to Matthew and me.

She was so shocked, she almost choked on her tea. She hinted that in her role, she was able to offer free training courses mental health first aid, ASIST but that CAMHS had told her such courses was not necessary as they were specialists, hiding behind titles in my eyes. As a youth worker working ethically with young people it would appear I had more mental health qualifications than CAMHS. When I left her, she was deep in thought?

I then met a gentleman from ZEST – a self-harm and suicide support agency and showed him that same first page. He read it assiduously, then, looking at me over his glasses said, 'Was Matthew diagnosed with Post Traumatic Stress Disorder?'

I frowned. 'No. My son wasn't diagnosed with any mental health disorder.'

'But he was referred to CAMHS?'

'Oh yes. Many times!' I relayed my experiences to him, and he listened intently.

'Hmm.' He looked annoyed. 'I have to tell you, Sharon, terrible though this is, I am not surprised.'

'You're not?'

'I've seen other, similar cases.'

And if that shocked me, and it did, what he said next came as a body blow.

'Don't be surprised,' he said, 'If the different services collude in order to prevent a court case.'

I stared at him, open mouthed as the penny dropped. I could imagine them all sitting round a boardroom table working out what they could write that would get me off their backs. 'They just hope I'll go away!' I said, and he nodded.

'Well that,' I said, 'it's simply not going to happen.'

And it wasn't. There was no way I was going to stop my investigation. Not when the suicide rate in Northern Ireland was on the increase. A fact brought home to me when one of Matthew's close friends Atlanta completed suicide a few months after he had died – an event that brought our community together as we sourced and shared information, finding out about all the local services who might help young people in distress. That strengthened my resolve.

Additional help came from an unexpected source. A year after Matthew had died, my dad contacted, asking if he could visit. I was reluctant to see him, and I told him so. 'It feels strange,' I said, 'that you want to see me now. I don't need a dad at 40 – I needed one when I was 10.'

He asked again, and I relented. Matthew's death had shown me that life is short, and maybe I should give him a chance. Perhaps he could add to my life?

He arrived, and we chatted. And, almost at once I recognised myself in him. We share mannerisms, and as I got to know him, I realised I got my sarcastic sense of humour from him too.

But the starkest realisation, was that he had this passion for fighting for justice. Working for the Royal Mail, he'd been a trade union representative, and in retirement, he clearly had a soft heart for those who needed looking after. And as we chatted, and I told him how I speak out at work, anxious to ensure that policy and procedure aims are met, he could see this same characteristic in me.

My dad wanted to fish in Antrim, but he needed a day license. We were told we could buy one from the old courthouse. We arrived there at 1.50pm and were told that the girl on the desk was at lunch but would be back by 2.00pm. So, we waited. As it happened, she didn't appear until nearer 3.00pm, and then told us that the courthouse no longer dealt with fishing licenses.

'You'll have to go over the road,' she said.

We walked over, only to find that the building had shut for the day just minutes before. 'That's frustrating,' I said. 'I hope that doesn't happen to many other people who want a license.'

He caught my eye, and we laughed.

'Right,' he said. 'Which of us is going to write that letter of complaint?'

It got us talking about CAMHS. And Dad said that he had seen situations like that many times before.

'Don't give up,' he said. 'Stick at this and you will win out.'

'You think so?'

He nodded. 'At the start of any dispute the people in an organisation stick together – anxious not to take the blame. But when they see how determined you are – and that you will not go away – their instinct for self-protection will kick in. That's when they start playing hot potatoes, passing the blame on to each other. Eventually someone will tell the truth.'

I saw the wisdom in his words, but still couldn't believe that professional adults in the mental health service would put a grieving mother through all this stress. 'I'm not going to sue them,' I said. 'That was never my intention. What would be the point? It wouldn't bring Matthew back.'

'I know,' he said, putting an arm round my shoulders.

'I want to make sure policies and procedures are followed,' I said. 'That's all. I want to ensure that they're doing the job they were set up to do. If they don't follow their aims and objectives, more teenagers will fall through the cracks. Especially when resources are so limited.'

Matthew's case was to be heard on 16th September 2015, in the coroner's court.
I was pleased. Now, hopefully I would learn the truth, but a week before the court date, the head psychiatrist wrote to the coroner's office amending his statement. He apologised for being unaware of Matthew's previous attempts on his life, stressing that he had not read about them in any notes. This simply wasn't true. It can't have been, since that information

was printed on the first page of Matthew's notes. Would he get away with, what to me, seemed a blatant lie?

The day came, and friends and family gathered round me for support. Terry came with me; so, did Mark; then there was Karen, Roberta, Darren; my sister Maria came, bringing along a friend, Vicky. And, most important, my solicitor, Niall Small. We faced the head psychiatrist and the social worker, along with the barristers for the Northern Trust.

I had two basic questions. Why did CAMHS not help Matthew and why did the head psychiatrist lie? And lie, deliberately, looking me straight in the eye? The coroner – a new one – felt that my questions were more suitable for a different court. At this news, my solicitor and their barristers got into discussion, and agreed that both sides would come up with statements to be read in court. These were read and rewritten until both sides were happy.

Here is my statement:

Matthew James Truesdale was born on 3rd April 1995. He was first and foremost a loving son. From the day he was born until the day he died family was important. Matthew was not only a son, he was a loving brother, nephew, grandson, friend and ultimately a father himself. When Matthew tragically died, he left behind a large devastated close family circle.

Unfortunately, Matthew didn't get to meet his child, but no one who ever knew Matthew would doubt he would have been an excellent father and true friend. Matthew had an excellent sense of humour which he shared with family and a large circle of friends.

He went to Antrim Primary School and then to Cambridge House and Park Hall College. Although extremely intelligent, Matthew didn't live long enough to achieve his ultimate goal of becoming a chef. He worked hard at school but enjoyed outside activities even more. He was often to be found fishing or in the gym.

Matthew was a beautiful child and an extremely handsome young man to the point that he worked part time as a model. Despite him being a 6ft2 muscular man those who knew him saw past this macho image to the warm sensitive gentle man who was afraid of spiders, the dark, or horror films, and loved nothing more than to spend time with his family.

During Matthews short life he was haunted by his own difficulties which he found difficult on occasions to cope with.

Despite these problems he struggled with, Matthew was clearly focused on his future to be a father learning to drive and fulfilling a career.

Matthew had many dreams, hopes and aspirations and his family are devastated at his untimely loss. We note the 19 learning points contained in the Serious Adverse Incident Report and hope the implementation of these will help prevent and support young men in the future.

The Northern Health Trust Statement

The Trust is committed to identification of learning from all incidents so as to inform continuous improvement and service provision.

A Serious Adverse Incident investigation was carried out by the Trust in respect of this tragic death. As a result of nineteen learning points were identified by the Trust and these are attached hereto.

Furthermore, the Serious Adverse Incident investigation, the conclusions and recommendations were subjected to independent review, the conclusions and recommendations from which are fully accepted, and the Trust is in the process of fully implementing those recommendations. The Trust shall keep Sharon Truesdale informed of the progress of this process in twelve months' time.

I had to be happy with that. And to an extent, I was. As Matthew's mother, I had done all I could, both physically and mentally, to have Mathew's death acknowledged, and for the Trust to highlight that they could have done more for him.

How I wished Matthew could come through the court doors and say, 'Well done, Ma! Now we can continue being a family.' Instead, I got his death certificate. But at least I now had a chance to grieve without the added stresses the struggle for justice had caused me.

The trust promised they would institute various training methods for their staff, and would let me know within a year, that the training was being implemented.

They sent me the list of 19 recommendations, as promised, but rather than gaining reassurance from the document, I felt horror that these basic safeguards had before now, been neglected. Training had been offered, but many of the staff failed to avail of it.

Reading the recommendations made me think back to the case of Madeline and Lauren O'Neill, back in 2005. Madeline had killed herself and her daughter just weeks after Madeline had received psychiatric care. Had the extensive report on her case been acted on? Or are they filed away and forgotten about?

All the recommendations about training for staff, to ensure they were competent in form filling, using history to identify behaviour patterns could take years to implement, but should already have been standard practice.

When I read that self-harm and suicide prevention training was recommended for staff, I caught my breath in fright. Surely, in this specialised agency that should be compulsory. Then I wondered if the implantation of the recommendations would have made any difference to Matthew. He spoke of his distress in clear terms. We both expressed fear for his future. What more could we have said to convince the agency to get Matthew the help he needed?

I have no doubt that those who worked with Matthew will remember him. My prayers are with those who did not do their job. To them I say, 'I forgive you, and pray that you can forgive yourself.'

All I can hope is that Matthews death may have improved the service. I will never know, but I trust that the staff are following policy and procedures so that no other mum, family, or community will have to suffer the way we have.

I'd expected the coroner's court to mark the end of my grieving – instead, it brought the horror of the past two years to the fore. I'd sit on his bed feeling stunned – sobbing, my heart aching – hit with the knowledge that Matthew was not going to walk through that door again. Not ever. How could I bear it?

To this day I haven't heard from the Northern Trust, and I suspect I will never know whether the changes that have been made, made a difference, or whether lessons have been learned.

I've had to learn, and accept, that I can't control what happens. I now know that I only have control over myself; over my feelings, behaviours and thoughts. I know that it's love, kindness and forgiveness that has got me through my grief. Firstly, showing this to me and then to others. I'm now able to move on and live the rest of my life.

13

Acceptance

I haven't forgotten Matthew, and I know I never will, but I can think of him with love, and remember the good times, without always focusing on the bad.

We've all comes to terms with it, as a family. Natasha's anger has been suppressed by good things in her life. Leaving school at 16, she worked in part-time jobs, before settling at a home for the elderly. She's happy there; good at a job she takes pride in.

It was funny when she went for the interview. She was surprised that they even offered her one.

'I messed up the application,' she told me, on the phone. 'It said complete it in black pen, and I used blue.' She laughed. 'And it said complete in capital letters, and I used small ones.'

If that was bad, she felt the interview went worse. 'Oh Mum, they asked me such stupid questions.'

'What sort of questions?'

'How do you know if an elderly person isn't well.'

'And what did you say to that?'

'That the person would tell you.'

I laughed.

'Well they would, wouldn't they? Anyway, they then asked me how I'd know if they didn't tell me.'

'And?'

'I said they'd be off their food or be pale.' She sighed. 'I really don't think I impressed them.'

When she rang me the next day, saying they'd offered her a job, she was ecstatic. 'They said they saw something in me!'

I was glad they could see beyond the blue hair, which was shaved on one side, and the tattoos acquired in memory of her brother. But they were right to. Natasha works with people who have dementia, and she loves it! She's been there for three years, and it's not an easy job. Often, she goes home covered in bruises because a patient has hit out at her. But she does have a way about her and is good at communicating with difficult patients.

There's one resident there who hadn't spoken for two years and known to be troublesome, and, perhaps, for that reason, Natasha, as a newcomer, ended up caring for them a lot – bathing and trying to persuade them to eat. She'd sit with them whenever she had a spare moment and after a while she broke through. Now they talk back. They let her feed them too, without the old battle. They look out for her, and his eyes light up when they catch sight of her.

They needed her and being needed has helped her to make sense of life after Matthew, just as my job, helping teenagers, has helped me.

When Mum was diagnosed with terminal cancer, back in May 2017, I was devastated. At 77 she was too young to die, and I wasn't ready to lose her, not for years! And how could I go through the painful journey I'd experienced with Matthew all over again?

My grieving started the minute the doctor uttered the word, 'terminal,' but when I'd had time to think it over, I thought, at least, after Matthew, I understood a little better how the process of death and grief worked. I held onto this thought hoping it was enough to save me from returning to my unhealthy ways for coping.

Then I realised it wouldn't be the same. Because at least her dying before me fulfilled an order of expectation. Like, the granny goes first then the mum. I certainly assumed I'd go before my children.

And with my mum we had more time to prepare. We had a lot of talks, and said everything we wanted to say, so when the time came there was no unfinished business. And that was part of Matthew's legacy. I'd learned, through his passing, all the things I needed to say, and I put all of that in place. Anything I needed to say, I said it. Not only to my mum but with each encounter with family and friends I wanted them to know that I love them and cherish our times together. Mindful that my life could end suddenly and unexpectedly; - in God's time.

There are still ifs and buts in my head surrounding Matthew's death. There always will be, but I'm more accepting that I didn't have any control over him, and I couldn't have prevented him from completing suicide. I don't have control over other people, and of how they behave; I only have control over myself.

I still have doubts about the doctors, but I've tried to let it all go. My mantra has become, 'Love and Kindness.' That's what I live by now. It's the lesson I've learned through the loss of Matthew. That and the art of forgiveness.

We all hoped that the doctors were wrong; that Mum would live to a better age, but her illness progressed fast, and in October she was taken into hospital. We'd visit every day – me, Natasha, and Annie-Jean. And sad though we were, I look back on those weeks with fondness. It was a precious time. We were lucky to have it. The two girls would sit beside their nana's bed for hours. Annie Jean brought her studies in. She would take her homework in and sit working whilst her nanna drifted in and out of sleep.

Natasha helped in more ways than one. She was pregnant with a baby due in November. Her partner, JT and she are well suited. They've been together now for years, and I knew they would make good parents. Mum was excited, and I knew would do everything in her power to stay alive long enough to meet her new great grandchild.

The doctors didn't see it like that. Whenever I saw one, as he checked Mum, he would take me to one side, and say, 'It'll be any day now.'

'It's all right,' I'd say, as if they were the ones who needed comforting. 'She'll be hanging on for the baby.'

Asking when the baby was due, hearing there were 16 days to go, the doctors would shake their heads in doubt. At least most of them would. But there was a lovely doctor from Coleraine who would always stop, and chat, as if he wasn't overworked, and didn't have to be in three places at once. When I told him my theory, he nodded, sagely.

'It doesn't make logical sense, but in my profession, seeing what I have seen, I would have to agree with you. I'm not making any promises, your mother is extremely unwell, but I would not be surprised if she hangs on for one or two days after the baby is born. She will be able to die content then. She will give herself permission.'

Every day I asked the nurses should I stay with Mum, and one evening they said that I should. 'We feel she might be near the end,' a nurse told me. 'She told the doctor that when she closed her eyes her bed was being pulled fast into a beautiful forest. And she mentioned 'seeing' the family and friends that she's lost.'

She was asleep when I arrived on the ward. I sat beside her, and after a while, I noticed that her eyes were open. 'Sharon,' she said. 'Who is that little boy with the blue shoes?'

Sitting up straighter, I looked around. Nobody was there, but Mum's eyes were fixed on a point beyond the foot of the bed, and I decided to humour her.

'I don't know, Mum. Who is he?'

'I don't know,' she said, as, slumping back on her pillow, she closed her eyes again.

The night went on. I sat there, beside Mum, dozing, when her voice rang out again. 'Sharon!' I jumped. 'Will you move out of the way.' She sounded angry. 'That lady needs to get behind you.'

I stood up, moved around for a while, then sat back down. I waited for her to object, but she'd moved on in her imaginary world, and was laughing and cajoling as if she was playing with someone.

'Mum? Who are you playing with?' This was bizarre!

'It's Alfie! The boy in the blue shoes is Alfie!'

I'd never heard of Alfie. But whoever he was, he had made my mum happy for the first time in days. She was wreathed in smiles, and I was pleased for her. For a while, I was pleased. But an hour later, when she began to tire, I felt that the interaction was bad for her. Besides, even if she didn't need her sleep, I did!

I began to silently pray. 'God, I don't know what is going on here. I don't know whether my mother is hallucinating, or whether she really can see somebody but please, this is not good for mum. Can you do something?'

Mum interrupted my prayer. 'Sharon, can you get me a tissue?'

I leant over, plucked one from the box on her locker, and passed it over.

'No, Sharon, I need three.'

Sighing, I plucked out two more.

'Alfie and his wee friends are crying,' she said. 'They say they need to go.'

I dropped the tissues in shock.

'You know who Alfie is?'

'No, mum. I don't.'

'That was my son,' she said. 'My stillborn son.'

Over the next few days, as she drifted in and out of consciousness, there were more incidences like that. She'd excuse herself and say she was in a meeting and talk in such a matter of fact way ,

'They told me last year,' she said, as if in response to a question. 'They said I had a diagnosis, and the diagnosis was cancer, and I didn't believe them. I said, 'Doctor, you're having a laugh!'

One time, she was talking in Chinese, something that we rarely witnessed unless in the local Chinese restaurant, to a favoured uncle who had passed a few years back.

It all seemed so plausible. So, when she told me that Matthew was there, standing beside me, I was open to the idea. I don't know where Matthew is, but I'm not scared anymore.

Natasha's due date arrived. She was admitted to hospital and given a pessary to induce her labour. We were all excited, but days went by, and nothing happened. On the Thursday, two days after the failed induction, they broke her waters. I was worried about leaving Mum, but when I popped up to the maternity ward, and took in the situation, I could see that JT needed a break.

He was deathly white, and was clearly distressed to see the state that Natasha was in. The contractions had begun now, and she was kept vomiting. Her heart rate was rising, and the nurses seemed worried. I sent JT off for half-an-hour and took over. JT was back in time to see Nancy enter the world, at six and a half pounds. It wasn't a straightforward birth – the cord was round Nancy's neck, and Natasha subsequently had a post-partum haemorrhage.

When the danger had eased, I went back to Mum's ward to tell the nurses I could now sit with Mum, but they took one look at me, and said, 'Sharon, go home!'

'It's a wee girl,' I said, and congratulating me, they said they already knew – they had heard from their colleague on the maternity ward.

The following day Mum was awake. I told her about little Nancy Louise, and showed her a photo, and played her a recording of the baby being born and crying. Then I showed her the video recording and she laughed.

'She's really beautiful,' I said, and she agreed. When I mentioned that she didn't look like her daddy, who has ginger hair, but was dark, like Natasha, mum said, 'Thank God!'

I laughed, then, seeing her shiver, asked her was she cold?

'I'm not cold,' she said, but that baby is cold. It's only got a nappy.' Then she fell asleep again.

Natasha and Nancy Louise went home on Thursday evening. They visited Mum before they left the hospital, and although she looked asleep, I know that made her so happy! They needed support the following night, and I said I would stay over with her. The following morning Paul, my brother-in law rang saying he was heading into the hospital, so I went home for a shower, before heading in to see Mum. But before I left home, Paul rang to say she had passed away.

I was devastated. I should have been there, and when I arrived at the hospital a nurse said they were so sorry I was not there, as they knew I didn't want Mum to pass on her own. I agreed, and said, 'I'm devastated.'

The doctor from Coleraine walked in, and seeing me, offered his condolences.

'And I wasn't there,' I said. 'She was all alone.'

'But she wouldn't have felt all alone,' he said. 'She was the one in control, and she was happy to go because she had seen her great-granddaughter.'

'Do you really think so?'

He nodded. 'It was her time. And she would have wanted you to be with Natasha.'

She was right. Mum had held on for two weeks. She'd had no food and existed on pain killers. But the minute she saw her granddaughter, and knew she had been named after her, she was at peace.

I went back to the fortune-teller the following February in Newcastle Upon Tyne. I never say anything to her; never tell her what has been going on in my life, so when she said, 'There has been a new baby born – a little girl,' I was impressed. I'd lost that initial scepticism.

'That's right,' I said. 'Her name's Nancy. She's Natasha's baby.'

She nodded. 'She's been sent to bring you joy, but there's so much sadness around this child. Your mummy has passed away. You look at the child sometimes, and it seems she is seeing someone beyond you.'

How did she know these things?

'You think she's playing with your mum.'

I sat still, determined not to give anything away.

'But she's not. She's playing with your son.'

I couldn't speak. Tears were coursing down my cheeks. Because I do feel Matthew around me sometimes. I know that's not logical. I believe that he's in heaven and that he's safe there. But sometimes I feel him and ask for a sign.

When Karen, Roberta, Tina and I went to Naples for a few days, I was thinking of Matthew. I didn't want to socialise with the others in the hostel and decided to go to bed early. Lying there, sleepless, I talked to Matthew in my head. I said, 'Matthew, if you are around me, I want a sign.'

I'd read that butterflies can indicate someone is around, but I see butterflies all the time. There had been the two pigeons, but they were plentiful too, so, thinking hard, I said, 'I want to see coins.'

All weekend, as we walked around, I spied the odd coin on the pavement, but that's normal – not a sign, and I woke on the last day with a sense of disappointment. Karen and I were standing at the bus station waiting to go to the airport when a taxi pulled up. A man climbed out, and all his loose change cascaded from his pocket. A two-euro piece fell right at my feet. That, I am convinced, was Matthew's sign to me.

14

Today

It is six years now since Matthew passed, and I'm still grieving. I don't believe that I will ever stop. Matthew was such a big part in my life, and he still is. He's there in the lovely memories I have of him. Grief, I have learned, cannot be 'fixed.' It has to be worked through.

I realise that everyone experiences grief differently, and I can't know how anyone else feels. But I'm sure my experience will resonate with people and help them, because there are bound to be commonalities.

My faith in God remains central to me. I continue to attend different churches, because I get a message each time I go. Sometimes, when I feel I don't fit in, or feel the ethos isn't truly Christian, I stop going for a while, and make my own form of worship, through prayer, reading, and listening to spiritual music. It always helps.

I wonder now if Matthew prayed. Did I do enough to pass on my faith? Did I talk about God enough? I remember, once, bribing the children with goldfish to attend church. Was that wrong? Did it have the opposite effect?

Matthew has taught me so much and made the person I am today. That's part of his legacy. He urged me to live life to the full, and to put myself first at times. 'You don't have to wrap the three of us in cotton wool,' he'd say. And, when Annie Jean's father, Mark and I had separated, he urged me to go and get myself another boyfriend. 'Or go out with your friends!'

My pregnancy with Daniel was high risk. The doctors were saying there was no guarantee that he would be born, so it was an intensely stressful time for me. Noticing my distress, Matthew said, 'What do the doctors know? Just pray, and things will be ok.' Those words made me feel so much better. And he was right; Daniel arrived safely.

When Matthew was still alive, I always felt a bit lost in my own life. I was Mum. It was, 'Ma do this,' or 'Mum do that.' I was always Mum to my children, and a daughter to my mother. I was a sister to my sister, and an auntie to my nephew. I think I lost 'me' in all that.

After Matthew – when I was struggling through my grief – I had to go back to basics, and to listen to my own needs. I had to put myself first sometimes. That could be hard, because people see you as being selfish.

When, for example, my sister said she was coming around at the weekend, and I said, 'No, not this weekend. I'm tired,' I felt was the worst in the world. You've been doing something for years, and suddenly, you're not. People can see you as self-centred, but all you're doing is looking after yourself.

I learned there is no shame looking after and putting me first thinking back to the analogy of oxygen masks in aeroplanes. I realised I needed to be ok in order to help others.

To do this, I had to learn that there's no shame in getting outside help. And although, sometimes, support groups or counselling didn't feel helpful, I had to remember that this might be because the time wasn't right. I learned to never turn my back on the idea.

Today, my life is good. I am happy! I'm working away. I've been working with young people now for 11 years; six of those with the education authority. I volunteer as a counsellor in Antrim and help with suicide intervention during heightened times in our community.

I think Matthew made me more passionate and a better youth worker. I'm more professional. I'm very strict about policy, and I struggle whenever it's not being followed. I'm like, 'it has to be done this way.'

There are times when the last thing I want to do in the evening is to go to a training workshop. But I remember Matthew and realise that, ethically, I have to go. I have to keep on top of things and I will strive on. I want to stay with the education authority, but I'd love to do more counselling. I would like to specialise in something, but I'm not sure of the speciality just yet.

I still cry and that's okay. I have learned to feel my emotions instead of trying to block or control them. I talk about Matthew whenever I feel the need, and I bring him into conversations. I've learned that it's okay to laugh too. When I laughed over the organ player at Matthew's funeral, I felt so guilty. It felt inappropriate at my son's funeral, but it was funny, and Matthew would have laughed.

I still receive a lot of support from my true friends – especially around those special dates, like Matthew's birthday and anniversary. But those who send flowers or cards on other days lift my spirits even more.

There's a lady Pamela who I worked with whose son Kyle knew Matthew. She has, twice, sent me a card saying she is thinking of me, and that meant so much.

Nothing stops the grieving process or takes the pain away, but it is all these small, kind gestures that make me feel valued, wanted and needed. They make all the difference in the world.

It's good to see Natasha so settled. And though she still doesn't see her dad, she has a new and good relationship with Jim – James's father. He, and his wife Jackie love baby Nancy Louise, and have welcomed her into the family. Natasha calls him Grandad, and, it turns out, Natasha and Jim have a lot in common. Both love horses, greyhounds, and the country life. They have become close, and it's been good for her, and has lessened the pain from the past.

It pleases me more than I can say, yet I don't resent James for his attitude. It's a choice, and we all have those. In the same way, it was Matthew's choice not to come into my room that last night and ask for help. It's something I simply have to accept. We are only in control of our own thoughts, behaviours and feelings.

My grandson, Matthew's son Tyler is five now. I look after him every Saturday, and he's best buddies with Daniel, who is now seven. Bronagh has a new partner, Aaron, and he seems nice. They have another wee boy, so Tyler has a little brother. He has a new family, but he hasn't forgotten about his daddy.

Recently Tyler said, 'I wish I had seen my daddy, Matthew,' and I said, 'You know your daddy Matthew did see you?'

'How did he see me, nanny Sharon?'

'When you were in your mummy's tummy, daddy Matthew went to a scan and there were photos of you.' He was pleased with that.

He knows that his daddy is in heaven, and he talks about him to Daniel. The other day the boys were in my car and Tyler said, 'My daddy says I'll be doing jujitsu soon.'

Daniel said, 'What? Your Daddy? Who *is* your daddy?'

'Daddy Aaron.'

And Daniel goes, 'But he's not your daddy. Your daddy is Matthew and he's in heaven.'

'Oh yeah,' said Tyler. 'I have two daddies Daddy Aaron and Daddy Matthew.'

A few months ago, he asked me how his daddy died. I wondered how I should answer that. I said, 'He wasn't well.'

'Why didn't you take him to the doctor, nanny Sharon?'

'I did,' I said, 'but the doctor couldn't help him.'

'Yeah, that's what Mummy said.'

I say the same to Daniel, but one day I will have to tell them exactly what happened to Matthew. I don't want them hearing from anyone else. I hope that Bronagh and I will continue to work together with an agreed narrative so that we are all saying the same thing to answer their questions as they grow older.

There were times when I really did not want to live. When the struggle to stay alive seemed just too great. But now I appreciate life and want to be around to see Daniel and Tyler growing up and to see baby Nancy Louise married.

There have been many people who have helped me through this difficult time, and some entered my life as a result of Matthew's death. All those people – the ones who I still see, and the ones I don't – have a place in my heart.

Last July, (2018) I had a health scare. Roberta my good friend and Rea, my sister in law had been diagnosed with cancer, and then Terry's sister in law died 14 weeks after a diagnosis. It was terrible. I saw an advertisement for free screening for bowels, breast and cervical cancer training, and, when a cruise I was due to go on was cancelled, I saw that as a sign that I should go. And I found it really valuable.

The following weekend, Roberta offered to take me to a hotel for the weekend. Before changing for dinner, I had a shower, and, remembering the course from the day before, I examined my breasts. And there it was. This lump.

The following morning, I rang the doctor and spoke to the receptionist who said someone would ring me back. We were in the car, driving home when the doctor rang, and I spoke to her in a kind of code, because I didn't want to worry my friend with my troubles – not when she had just been through her own cancer.

The doctor asked me to go in the following day. She felt the lump, but said she was confident that it was nothing to worry about. 'But I'll flag it up as urgent,' she said. 'You'll be hearing from the hospital within two weeks, or, if you don't hear soon, you could ring them in a week.'

The hospital rang as I was walking through my front door. 'Can you come in next week?' the receptionist asked, and I said I could. But I was sick with worry, and my mood sank into my boots. I didn't talk to anyone about it, but I planned how I'd would, later, tell everyone my terrible news. Because I was convinced, I had cancer. They would tell me so at my appointment. If they didn't strongly suspect it, why had they rung so soon?

I had a mammogram, and then a biopsy. Then I was called in for a diagnosis. The doctor was smiling. 'It's swollen glands,' she said, and I breathed out, the tension leaving my body.

Driving home, feeling a lightness, I thanked God that I didn't have cancer. Then a sense of annoyance took over. Why had I convinced myself the news would be bad, and wasted all those hours in worry? Worry about dying, but anxiety at my unpreparedness too.

It taught me a lesson. I would plan for my death, so that if I had another scare, I wouldn't face any unnecessary worry. I reviewed my will, making sure Tyler and Nancy Louise would be included, and I planned my funeral. And then, in September, we were in a car accident. We were, thankfully, all right, but it shook me.

I really want to live now. I tell Daniel I will live until I'm 100, because I love certificates, and want to get one from the Queen.

Epilogue

This is the first time I have opened up and spoke about my real experiences. I am a private person and the inspiration for writing my story is the hope that it will provide comfort and support to anyone affected by suicide, grief or mental health. And to help break the stigma.

I'd like to end this book with a summary of all that Matthew's death has taught me. The tragic loss of my son has caused me 'a broken pain' that follows me in life. During this journey it felt my life was overwhelmed with people including the police, doctors, taking over. Together with 'grief' I was lost.

A low mood which resulted in a loss of interest in doing things that I enjoyed, unable to sleep because of flashbacks and nightmares, forgetting to eat because I had difficulty remembering or concentrating, doing things that didn't make sense and hearing and seeing things no one else can led me to believe that I was going mad and if I shared this with anyone they would lock me up and throw away the key.

If I had to give just one piece of advice, it would be this; talk to someone. During times when I was feeling really low it helped me to talk to my friends even if I had to drag myself out of bed, it was important not to be alone.

Good friends were a godsend to me. Especially the ones who gave me practical help; who did the shopping or turned up with a cooked meal or sandwiches. The best friends listened to me for hours but were never judgemental. They were patient and understanding. Some talked through the things that had helped them in times of distress; like breathing exercises, or walking. They encouraged me to break the cycle of grief and establish a better routine. They reminded me of the things I had liked to do before Matthew's death. I appreciated every form of contact. Even a text message could lift my day and show someone was thinking of me.

The old confident Sharon Truesdale who spent her life never showing real emotions to anyone, the logical one, the friend who you go to for advice found it difficulty to be truly honest and open to friends. I didn't lie but I didn't share the whole truth how I was feeling so finding a counsellor was really helpful. As the trusting relationship developed, I could be my true self sharing my real feelings, thoughts and behaviours. The process allowed me to make sense of what was happening and helped me to start take back control of me and my life. It was shocking to realise that it took nine months of weekly counselling before I accepted my son had died.

I had never been on anti-depressant medication before, and the first time I tried them they made me sick. But after a month, using an online meditation tool too, my sleep began to improve. I slept for five to six hours a night and began to feel okay. I am still taking an anti-depressant today.

There were days that I wanted to stay in bed; when the thought of getting up, let alone dressing and making the dinner felt like a step too far. I pushed myself to shower, dress and look presentable each day, whether or not I was going out. I kept a diary and made myself accomplish something every day. It could be, simply opening a letter, and I made myself eat three meals a day, go for a walk, and go to bed, even though that meant facing my fears. After a while I felt a sense of achievement in that and my mood improved.

I read books and started to learn about mindfulness, living in the here and now. That was hard. I'd walk to get away from my grief, but my mind would keep returning to Matthew, and I'd relive those terrible first weeks. I'd watch films with friends but find my thought drifting. But with practise, I learned to stay tuned with nature, or with the film.

I learned to listen to me by showing myself love, kindness and forgiveness. By listening to my thoughts, feelings and noticing the behaviour I attributed to them I was able to make positive changes which allowed me to take control. During times of panic I would colour in books and practice breathing exercises. And when life was really bad, I'd voice my suicidal thoughts. I'd say, to Terry, 'I feel as if I don't want to be here.' Just being able to tell him made me feel better.

I made myself get out and be social. I accepted that I was grieving and I needed time to deal with the loss of my son and take time to look after me and my family. I'd take Daniel to the park and get out and visit friends. I'd remember the old Sharon Truesdale and try and act the way she had although I know that part of her died the same day as Matthew.

I made myself get up at 7.20am. I started watching the films and programmes I'd once watched with Matthew, doing all the things he would like to think if me doing. I watched Breaking Bad, and Dexter on Netflix,

I now talk about Matthew without shame. If someone asks me how many children, I include him, and then explain the situation if appropriate, no longer scared of being defined as the mother who lost her son through suicide because I am so much more. I discuss the special memories I have of him. When someone mentions Matthew, it helps me. I am thinking about him all the time, and it's good to know that others are thinking of him too.

I gave myself permission to grieve. I'd say to myself, 'I'm sad today, but it's because I'm grieving, and that's natural. I am going to be okay!' I give myself positive affirmations. I repeat, 'I am a good mother. I did everything I could.' I've learned to treat myself as I like to treat others, with love, kindness and forgiveness, and slowly, I've learned to cope better.

Everyone told me that the first year would be the hardest. That may be true for most people, but my grief was even worse during the second year. It came to a head when I attended the coroner's court and realised that this was not a dream. Matthew wasn't coming back.

As a mum, counsellor and a youth worker, it's important to share that Matthew did not want to die. He was planning his eighteenth birthday party and looking forwards to the birth of his son. His death had a devastating effect on me, on his siblings, friends and community. Although Matthew ended his pain, he transferred it onto all those who knew and loved him when he completed suicide.

Holding onto my faith has helped me. There is a verse in the bible Isaiah 40:10, 'Fear thou not; for I am with thee: be not dismayed; for I am thy God: I will strengthen thee; yea, I will help thee; yea, I will uphold thee and with the right hand of my righteousness.' That gives me great comfort. In the early days, when I lay in bed, scared to close my eyes, let alone try to sleep, I'd imagine myself as a little girl holding onto Jesus's hand. I still do that sometimes. It reassures me that I am not alone.

It's important that everyone gets support for their mental health. There is support out there; a friend, your GP, an organisation who will be able to give you the help and support that you need to live your life. One day your story will inspire and give someone the strength and support they need. And together we will break the stigma.

HELPFUL ORGANISATIONS IN NORTHERN IRELAND

Aware Defeat Depression	02890 357820
Barnardo's Child Bereavement Support Service	02890 668333
Childline	0800 1111
Compassionate Friends	02887 788016
Cruse Bereavement support	02890 792419
Lifeline:	0808 808 8000*
Lighthouse Charity	02890 755070
NHSCT Bereaved by Suicide Service	02894 413544
Samaritans:	116 123
Wave Trauma Centre	02890 779922
Zest NI	02871 266999

- Lifeline counsellors are available 24 hours a day and phone calls are free from mobiles or landlines calling from UK.

Made in the USA
Columbia, SC
04 August 2019